Shylock, the Roman

Robert Schneider

Shylock, the Roman
Unmasking Shakespeare's
The Merchant of Venice

by Robert Schneider

PULPLESS.com, inc.
775 East Blithedale Ave., Suite 508
Mill Valley, CA 94941, USA.
Voice & Fax: (500) 367-7353
Home Page: http://www.pulpless.com/
Business inquiries to info@pulpless.com
Editorial inquiries & submissions to
editors@pulpless.com

PULPLESS.com, inc.

First Pulpless.Com™, Inc. Edition August, 1999.
Library of Congress Catalog Card Number: 99-61048
ISBN: 1-58445-066-5

Book and Cover designed by CaliPer, Inc.
Cover Illustration by Billy Tackett, Arcadia Studios
© 1999 by Billy Tackett
Author's Photo by Lewis Bushnell
© 1999 by Lewis Bushnell

To my wife, Christine, who inspired me to persist in explicating a play that celebrates absolute fidelity in a world of deceptive appearances, where extreme opposites converge and are inevitably misperceived.

Table of Contents

We should hold day with the Antipodes,
If you would walk in absence of the sun.
The Merchant of Venice, 5.1.127-128[1]

Transitional beyond many eras, mingling divided and distinguished worlds, the Shakespearian age witnessed numerous revaluations and reversals. Not unexpectedly, a favourite metaphor was the 'world upside down.'   —W.R. Elton[2]

Preface

Appearances are deceptive. Most people will agree with this statement—that superficial appearance can be misleading. Nevertheless, most people continue to be deceived by superficial appearances. For example, people don't believe that personal appearance should have anything to do with competence, but research continues to show that most people believe that a handsome man is more trustworthy than an ugly one, and that a tall person is more likely to be viewed as an effective manager or leader than someone who is short. Most women understand clearly how powerful—for better or worse—personal appearance can be. We like it when the good guys wear the white hats, and the bad guys wear the black—when people who look good are good, noble and trustworthy, when ugly people are liars, thieves and generally bad. White and black hats simplify matters. They enable us to believe that we are getting to the root of the matter quickly.

We all make superficial judgments, but we'd rather credit ourselves with the intelligence and expertise to grasp reality quickly rather than to admit that we make superficial judgments based on preconceived notions and prejudices; however, when other people make this mistake, we easily understand that they are illogical and short-sighted. We don't like to admit that we are too lazy to look beneath superficial appearance, even though that might be the case quite often.

Businesses understand this fact of human nature, and invest hundreds of billions of dollars in advertising on the assumption that people will make significant decisions based upon superficial information. People buy luxury cars for tens of thousands of dollars and computer networks for tens of millions of dollars based on little more than a brand image, derived primarily from advertising. Brand image convinces people that there is a great difference between drinks as similar as Coca-cola and Pepsi-cola. It convinces people to pay significantly more for a product that may have only a single advantage over similar products—a designer label.

Like corporations, politicians and political organizations also understand that people don't have the patience to study issues deeply; they may feel passionately about major issues, but don't care enough to examine the details. They simply want to know who wears the white hat and who wears the black. President Bill Clinton is a good example of the strength of a brand image. He has succeeded in positioning himself as standing for compassionate, caring and enlightened government, which he contrasts with the negative image of his enemies, who are positioned as intolerant, right wing zealots who want to impose their narrow beliefs on everyone else. Consequently, feminists have been Clinton's staunchest defenders despite considerable proof of his contempt for the sexual harassment laws that he has sworn to uphold; apparently feminists believe sexual harassment laws are not important enough to require that defendants either testify truthfully or suffer penalties. The same people who said Clarence Thomas wasn't fit to serve on the Supreme Court vigorously defended President Bill Clinton, even though there is far more evidence that Clinton, not Thomas, has been a predator who will either help a woman's career or attack her reputation depending upon whether or not she has granted him a sexual favor. Put another way: Thomas is a short, black man whose conservatism feminists consider to be a black hat; Clinton is a tall, white man who brags about wearing a white hat. The specific facts may be against Clinton, but the strength of his brand image defines how those facts are interpreted. Likewise, Paula Jones is not a "beautiful person," while Hillary Clinton is blond and eloquent. Most people will find Hillary more credible than Paula, even though Paula may be the one who told the truth about this case.

There is an important kernel of truth at the heart of the story of the "Emperor's New Clothes." We assume that the Emperor is foolish for believing that his tailors are the best in the world even though he cannot see any clothes with his own eyes. We would prefer to think that we would be like the child who speaks up and says what's obvious. However, we are not inclined to learn the lesson of the story: that our preconceptions—our beliefs, our prejudices—determine what we see, not our eyes. We are all Emperors wearing new clothes, because unlike children, we carry with us the heavy cultural baggage of preconceptions and prejudices; and we don't appreciate it when someone presumes to tell us that we have no clothes. When we look in the mirror, we don't see actual clothes; we see a reflection of our own ego, our deepest held beliefs about ourselves, our families, our country.

Appearances determine our perception of reality. This point is not trivial; it is basic to the human condition. We project our inner selves onto the outside world, which is why we are not inclined to notice when the facts do not correspond to our beliefs. We think we know the difference between appearance and reality, but fundamentally our expectations shape what we see, and we are comfortable with the notion that appearance is an accurate representation of reality. When the issues at hand mean a great deal to us—politics, religion, appreciation for the arts—it is easy to see how people will be in the thrall of their own passionate beliefs and less inclined to be open to another perspective. That is also why we are inclined to perceive the mistakes of others before we recognize our own fallibilities; hypocrisy, along with the tendency to be deceived by superficial appearance, is also basic to the human condition.

The Merchant of Venice has been a lightening rod for highly emotional, ego-driven controversy. The play introduces certain stereotypes that draw forth the prejudices and preconceived notions of readers and theater-goers alike. The play's most superficial elements stimulate an intensely passionate response that makes it difficult to get to the bottom of the play's meaning. This response is part of the play's meaning, which concerns the issues of appearance and reality, deceptiveness and sincerity, hypocrisy and honor. In a word, *The Merchant of Venice* is a play about the deceptiveness of superficial appearance that is itself deceptive at a superficial level.

Just as many people bring considerable cultural baggage to the experience of reading or seeing *The Merchant of Venice,* many readers will give a book like *Shylock, the Roman* only a superficial glance because their minds are—for the most part—made up already. In general, people want to read something that will cater to their preconceptions about Shakespeare and *The Merchant of Venice.* Scholars are not expecting any breakthrough insight that "could alter, even revolutionize, our understanding of the loftiest figure in the history of English literature."[3] The consensus today is that "while it is certain that every age will produce its own interpretations, its own Shakespeare, it grows less and less likely that someone will come up with some sort of archaeological find, a riddle answered."[4] Nevertheless, great literature has an uncanny resilience that persistently defies what we think we already know. "When you read a canonical work for a first time," Harold Bloom says in *The Western Canon:*

> You encounter a stranger, an uncanny startlement rather than a fulfillment of expectation.... One mark of an originality that can win

canonical status for a literary work is a strangeness that we either never altogether assimilate, or that becomes such a given that we are blinded to its idiosyncrasies.[5]

The Merchant of Venice, in this light, exactly fulfills Bloom's definition of canonical literature as a work of "uncanny startlement, rather than a fulfillment of expectations." It is a work of unique "strangeness" that has never been assimilated properly, even as we have become "blinded to its idiosyncrasies."[6] In other words, *The Merchant of Venice* is a play for which "the outward shows be least themselves. / The world is still deceived with ornament" (*MV*, 3.2.73-74).

Introduction

The two faces of Portia: honor and irony

There has been a fairly wide spectrum of opinion about *The Merchant of Venice*, which—even after 400 years or so—continues to provoke controversy and debate.[7] Nevertheless, throughout 400 years of performance and discussion, one fundamental premise has remained constant and unchallenged despite the diversity of interpretation otherwise: the play's moral perspective has always been defined by a Christian/Jewish moral paradigm. This basic premise has shaped the way the play has been interpreted for 400 years. Simply put, the conflict between Antonio (the merchant) and Shylock (the Jewish money lender) has set the stage for interpretations that assume a clash between Christian love and Jewish law, mercy and vengefulness, New Testament and Old.

Shylock, the Roman challenges this basic premise. The text of the play remains unchanged, of course. But when that text is perceived in terms of a different interpretive paradigm, the fundamental meaning of one of Shakespeare's better-known plays changes in an unprecedented way. This approach—discovering something new by framing "old" facts in a fresh context—is similar to the method employed in *The Purloined Letter* by Edgar Allan Poe's detective, C. Auguste Dupin. Dupin quickly solves the mystery of the missing letter, but his foil, the "Prefect of the Parisian police," remains baffled because his preconceptions preclude his finding the letter, even if it isn't hidden at all. The difference between a simple solution and confusing complexity is not to be found in the facts of the case, which remain constant. The distinction between fore-

ground and background—between the obvious and the obscure, the open and the opaque, the explicit and the implicit,
the self-evident and the enigmatic—is to be found, as Dupin
understands quite well, in the interpretive paradigm through
which the basic facts are perceived. So it is with interpretations of *The Merchant of Venice*. The key that unlocks a new
meaning for *The Merchant of Venice* is not buried deeply in the
most obscure nook; neither is the revelation of anything previously undiscovered necessary for the discovery of an entirely
new meaning to a thoroughly familiar play. Instead, like
Dupin's solution to the mystery of the purloined letter, the play's
meaning is "hidden" out in the open, where it has been all
along, where one would least expect to find it.

It must be granted at the outset that there is no obvious reason why a new paradigm would be useful to an interpretation
of *The Merchant of Venice*. The play's central conflict is a dis-
pute between Christian and Jew: the play's Christians ask Shylock, the Jewish money lender, to show mercy to Antonio, the
Christian merchant, who has failed to meet the terms of
Shylock's loan. But despite their pleas, Shylock cruelly insists
upon the letter of the law and demands a pound of Antonio's
flesh. This conflict is both powerful and prominent; its importance would seem to require that the play be interpreted from
within the traditional Christian/Jewish perspective.

Here is the play in brief: Shylock, the Jew, lends Antonio
money, which Antonio in turn lends to his friend Bassanio,
who needs this financial support to court Portia, a wealthy
heiress. In order to win Portia's hand, Bassanio must correctly
choose one of three small treasure chests, which are made of
gold, silver and lead respectively. He correctly chooses the casket of lead. However, Antonio suffers a business setback and
is unable to meet the terms of his contract with Shylock. Shylock then demands a pound of Antonio's flesh, which is the
penalty stipulated by the terms of their agreement. Portia—in

disguise as Balthasar, a legal expert—elevates the legal question to the higher plane of morality: she asks that Shylock show mercy to Antonio, speaking of mercy as heavenly, as an attribute of God Himself. When Shylock demands a judgment on the basis of temporal law rather than divine compassion, Portia is able to save Antonio by holding Shylock to the exact letter of his bond, threatening him with penalties if he takes the least bit more or less than the pound of flesh stipulated in the bond. It is not surprising that Shylock and Portia have been identified with Jewish legalism and Christian salvation respectively.

There are other plot elements in the play: Shylock's servant, Lancelot Gobbo, leaves Shylock's household to work for Bassanio. Shylock's daughter, Jessica, escapes from home to marry a Christian, Lorenzo. Bassanio's man, Graziano, courts Portia's lady-in-waiting, Nerissa. And Bassanio and Graziano give away to Portia and Nerissa (who are in disguise) rings that they had promised never to part with. However, the conflict between Antonio and Shylock, more than any other plot element, has traditionally defined the play's themes in moral terms derived from a Christian/Jewish interpretive paradigm: mercy versus revenge, generosity versus greed, love versus hatred, and ultimately, New Testament morality versus Old Testament morality, Christian versus Jew. Interpretations of the play have fallen somewhere within the scope of these antithetical moral extremities.

Shylock, the Roman reframes *The Merchant of Venice* in terms of an alternative to the Christian/Jewish paradigm—the honor/irony paradigm. The conflict between Antonio and Shylock remains important to any interpretation of the play, but from the perspective of the honor/irony paradigm, this conflict represents something more complex than a clash between Christian ideal and Jewish stereotype. Instead of the traditional Christian/Jewish themes, the honor/irony approach to the play focuses on themes related to the confusion of appearance and reality: deception and honor; comic irony and quotidian morality; relativistic perspective and absolutistic faith.

The moral terms of the honor/irony paradigm are defined by two antithetical extremes derived from classical culture:

- The Elizabethan ideal of ancient Roman honor, which is serious, self-restrained and elitist.
- The festive immorality of ancient Roman comedy that is ancient Roman honor's moral antithesis—frivolous, self-indulgent and populist.

Ancient Roman honor is sincere and straightforward, while ancient Roman comedy thrives upon festive irony, disguises and deceptions.

The conflicting antitheses of honor and irony have their metaphor in the "two faces of Portia." There are only two characters named "Portia" in all of Shakespeare's work—one in *Julius Caesar*, the other in *The Merchant of Venice*. These two characters personify the two antithetical faces of Portia: tragic honor and comic irony. In *Julius Caesar*, a tragic Portia commits suicide in a gruesome way; she has "swallowed fire" (IV.iii.156),[8] according to Brutus, her husband, who himself later commits suicide after suffering political and military defeats.[9] This Portia (broadly speaking) represents personal integrity according to the ancient Roman concept of honor. In contrast, in *The Merchant of Venice*, a comic Portia takes matters of personal integrity more lightly, joking with her husband about his broken promise never to part with his fidelity ring and then living happily ever after with him. The comic Portia herself has two faces: the first, a disguise as Balthasar, a "young doctor of Rome" (4.1.152) who is the judge who rules on Shylock's claim to a pound of flesh; the second, her "real" self: a woman engaged in romantic courtship. Taken together, the two faces of the comic Portia represent an ironic inversion of the ideals exemplified by the tragic Portia. This comic Portia represents festive irony (broadly speaking) because of her dramatic function within the context of the play.

The term "paradigm" is something of a cliché, especially in the business world today. In proposing a new paradigm for *The Merchant of Venice*, "paradigm" is used in the manner defined by the late Thomas S. Kuhn in his seminal work, *The Structure of Scientific Revolutions*:

> On the one hand, it [a paradigm] stands for the entire constellation of beliefs, values, techniques, and so on shared by the members of a given community. On the other, it denotes an element in that constellation, the concrete puzzle-solutions which, employed as models or examples, can replace explicit rules as a basis for the solution of the remaining puzzles of normal science.[10]

Kuhn considers the first sense of the term sociological. The second sense, which he calls "the deeper of the two," defines paradigms "as exemplary past achievements,"[11] such as those of Copernicus, Newton, Lavoisier and Einstein. Each of these individuals:

> necessitated the community's rejection of one time-honored scientific theory in favor of another incompatible with it. Each produced a consequent shift in the problems available for scientific scrutiny and the standards by which the profession determined what should count as an admissible problem or as a legitimate problem-solution. And each transformed the scientific imagination in ways that we shall ultimately need to describe as a transformation of the world within which scientific work was done. Such changes, together with the controversies that almost always accompany them, are the defining characteristics of scientific revolutions.[12]

Paradigms in this sense are "universally recognized scientific achievements that for a time provide model problems and solutions to a community of practitioners."[13]

One example of a sociological or cultural paradigm that defines a community's world view is the ancient Roman cultural paradigm, which includes both the ethos of Roman honor and the festive irony of Roman comedy (characterized here as the

two faces of Portia.) One might also speak of the paradigm of
Roman comedy, although from a higher-level perspective, Roman comedy is only one component of a more widely-encom-
passing paradigm, that of ancient Roman culture, which includes both festive license and normative restraint. The Elizabethan world view represents another sociological paradigm,
which encompasses cultural influences derived both from
pagan Greco-Roman culture and from Christian tradition. In
this context, the ancient Roman cultural paradigm is a subset
of the Elizabethan cultural paradigm, within which classical
Latin literature is an important component, though obviously
not the only component.

Shylock, the Roman is intended to be a new paradigm in
Kuhn's more significant sense, that of a problem/solution
model. This new interpretation of *The Merchant of Venice* does
not discover new information as much as it advocates, as Kuhn
said, "a change in the perception and evaluation of familiar
data."[14] It proposes a new solution to an old problem, but does
so by first displacing the old problem with an entirely new
one—a problem that hasn't previously been recognized as significant, namely: What is the relationship between the obscure
references to ancient Roman culture in the play's background
and the obvious references to Christian/Jewish morality in its
foreground?

There is a basic contradiction between the Christian/Jew-
ish themes in the foreground and the Roman honor/irony
themes in the background. On the one hand, Portia invokes
the ideal of Christian mercy when she confronts Shylock; but
on the other hand, Portia's legal rationale (which deflects
Shylock's claim to Antonio's flesh) is shown to be an inversion
of ancient Roman law, in the pattern of ancient Roman
comedy's festive irony. On the surface, Portia stands for Christian morality, but less obviously, she also represents the festive immorality of the Roman carnival, which is fundamen-

tally antithetical to Christian morality. To be sure, the play celebrates mercy, but there is a great deal of difference between Christian mercy and mercy in the context of Roman comedy and festive immorality. The play's obvious Christian foreground and obscure Roman background are complementary in one sense, but contradictory in another.

The point is not that the play appears to be "about" Christian morality, but is instead *"really* about" ancient Roman honor. Neither is it the point that some other, secret meaning lies behind the play's ostensibly obvious meaning. The significance of the honor/irony paradigm lies in its reciprocal relationship with the traditional Christian/Jewish paradigm. The play frequently and explicitly states that obvious appearances are misleading, that they misrepresent the truth. This theme is clear and obvious throughout the play, notably in a major speech that begins: "So may the outward shows be least themselves./ The world is still deceived with ornament" (3.2.73-74). Bassanio's speech concludes that superficial appearance is: "The seeming truth which cunning times put on/ To entrap the wisest" (3.2.100-101). This insight—that superficial appearance *least* resembles the actual fact of the matter—enables Bassanio to win Portia's hand in marriage by correctly selecting the ugly casket made of lead, rather than the more attractive caskets of gold and silver.

The fundamental meaning of *The Merchant of Venice* is not hidden at all. The play is about the deceptiveness of what appears to be obvious. That message is reiterated in many ways throughout the play. What could be more obvious? And at the same time, what could be more deceptive? This approach ultimately leads to a self-reductive conclusion: that the obvious and ostensibly self evident meaning of *The Merchant of Venice* is deceptive because—according to *The Merchant of Venice*—superficial appearances are deceptive. In effect, *The Merchant of Venice*—a play about the deceptiveness of appearance—is itself deceptive in appearance, even as it openly declares that appearances are deceptive.

The traditional approach to the play is ultimately reductive to beliefs about Christian mercy and Jewish justice that are external to the play; and a polemical religious perspective would be an exception—not the rule—to the pattern of Shakespearean drama. When it is interpreted in terms of the quasi-theological perspective of the traditional Christian/Jewish paradigm, *The Merchant of Venice* runs against the grain of Shakespeare's other work. In contrast, the honor/irony approach is not reductive to any concept or ideal external to the play itself. It is self-reductive: it is about that which it says it is about, and is reductive ultimately to the irony that is fundamental to its genre.

The honor/irony paradigm is non-traditional in so far as *The Merchant of Venice* is concerned, but its perspective is completely within the mainstream of traditional scholarship in the broader context of Shakespeare's other work. It maps "the hidden roads"[15] between *The Merchant of Venice* and other Shakespeare plays and sources, especially a subset of the plays written (along with *The Merchant of Venice*) in an approximately five-year period beginning in 1595 and ending in 1600, in the second quarter of Shakespeare's 20-year career. These play's include: *A Midsummer Night's Dream* (1595), *Romeo and Juliet* (1595), *The Taming of the Shrew* (1596), *Much Ado About Nothing* (1598/1599), *Julius Caesar* (1599) and *As You Like It* (1599/1600), as well as *Coriolanus* (1608/1609) and *Othello* (1605). Similarly, the honor/irony paradigm closely examines the connections between Shakespeare's plays and Plutarch's *Lives of the Noble Romans*, in the translation by Sir Thomas North (1579)—"the source that inspired him [Shakespeare] most."[16] The common points of reference between *The Merchant of Venice* and these other works bring focus to a mutually reinforcing web of insight.

The honor/irony problem/solution model challenges some of the overly simplistic thematic dichotomies typical of the Christian/Jewish paradigm; and at the same time simplifies some of the complexities and contradictions that have been typical of traditional *Merchant of Venice* interpretation. This new approach to the play at first seems obscure, but becomes clearer and more obvious as its various pieces fall into place. That will happen chapter by chapter, beginning first with an examination of some basic premises.

Cultural paradigms, critical premises

In the final scene of *Hamlet*, the mortally wounded Prince of Denmark asks Horatio to tell his story: "Horatio, I am dead./ Thou livest; report me and my cause aright/ To the unsatisfied." Horatio replies: "Never believe it./ I am more an antique Roman than a Dane./ Here's yet some liquor left" (*Ham.*, V.ii.323-327). There's no time for a lengthy explanation as Hamlet lies dying. By referring to himself as an antique Roman, Horatio quickly and clearly tells Hamlet that he intends to commit suicide on the basis of his commitment to a code of honor derived from the example of noble ancient Romans.

Study of the pagan classics—such as Plutarch, a major source of material for Shakespeare's *Coriolanus, Antony and Cleopatra, Julius Caesar* and *Timon of Athens*—was a special source of spiritual nourishment for aristocratic gentlemen, who sought to emulate the models of literary style and moral rectitude that they found in ancient history, literature and philosophy. They took their standards for honor and nobility from the examples of "the ancients," who (in their eyes) had attained a level of nobility that could only rarely (if ever) be equaled by any "moderns." Contemporary "moderns" were assumed to be superficial and self-serving, particularly in comparison to the integrity and depth of character attributed to the ancients,

an assumption that is evident in a comment made by Orlando
in *As You Like It*:

> O good old man, how well in thee appears
> The constant service of the antique world,
> When service sweat for duty, not meed!
> Thou are not for the fashion of these times,
> Where none will sweat but for promotion.   (*AYL*, II.iii.56-60)

Latin language and classical culture were the basis for whatever education anyone had in Shakespeare's day.[17] "Classical
knowledge was ubiquitous, and all educated people shared its
terms," A.L. Rowse writes:

> Classical knowledge is something different from the pedantry of
> scholarship .... In the Elizabethan age—a Renaissance age—the clas-
> sical world was all round one, in towns, streets, painted signs, heral-
> dic arms, reliefs on chimney pieces, in furniture, even tombs; ren-
> dered in plaster-work, painted glass, wall paintings, tapestries,
> needlework, cushions, arras hangings; pictures like that of Elizabeth
> I astounding the three Graces ...[18]

In the cultural milieu of Elizabethan England, ancient Roman honor was a relatively familiar concept, even to those
who were not classical scholars. It was an ideal that comple-
mented Christian tradition within the mainstream of Renaissance culture, even though Roman morality and Christian
morality are antithetical in some respects. For example, in direct contrast to Christianity's emphasis on personal humility
and turning the other cheek, the ethos of ancient Rome could
justify suicide or murder in defense of personal honor (as it
did in *Hamlet*, for example, or for Brutus in *Julius Caesar*).
"The Roman praise of suicide [as] an act of moral courage and
nobility ...[is] an attitude very different from Christian belief."[19]
According to Professor Maurice Charney:

> The foremost defining element for the Roman character in
> Shakespeare is the willingness to commit suicide rather than live
> ignobly or suffer death by another hand. All the suicides in the Ro-

man plays are presented as a proof of virtue.[20]

For Shakespeare, suicide is a "characteristically Roman act." However, "from a Christian point of view," Charney notes, "suicide is a sin against the Holy Spirit.... Shakespeare seems to have separated the Roman from the Christian attitude."[21] Nevertheless, these two moralities—Christian and ancient Roman—though antithetical in some ways, share a puritanical moral tone; they are identical in their disdain for superficial pleasures and self-indulgence. These two traditions, despite their differences, together established a foundation for Western European culture in the Renaissance.

In the 400 years since *The Merchant of Venice* was first performed in the 1590s, its context for interpretation has been defined by the Christian side of the Elizabethan cultural equation, as if Western civilization were based on a monogenetic moral tradition that is purely Christian. Traditional criticism has focused on themes derivative of a Christian/Jewish interpretive paradigm, within which matters relating to the ancient Roman moral perspective are not relevant. This cultural astigmatism is not surprising, considering that the conflict between Antonio and Shylock is certainly of central importance to the play's meaning. Consequently, the play has been interpreted as a clash of antithetical values derived from a Christian/Jewish paradigm: mercy versus revenge, friendship versus law, love versus hate, New Testament charity versus Old Testament justice—a variety of themes that are derived from the conflict of Jew versus Christian.[22]

Although no one has questioned the fundamental Christian/Jewish interpretative paradigm, some critics have emphasized the play's religious content more than others.[23] For example, C.L. Barber, in his important and influential book, *Shakespeare's Festive Comedy*, contends that the play represents the transcendence of Christian law, of the new covenant, the New Testament, over the Old. Barbara K. Lewalski makes a similar point:

> The Shylock-Antonio opposition functions...at what the medieval theorists would call the "allegorical" level; in these terms it symbolizes the confrontation of Judaism and Christianity as theological systems—the Old Law and the New—and also as historic societies.[25]

Writing in *Shakespeare Quarterly*, John S. Coolidge summarizes this perspective:

> *The Merchant of Venice* is the one play of Shakespeare which can be called a work of Christian apologetics ... only in *The Merchant of Venice* does he make an expressly Christian argument the basis for an entire play.[26]

Nevertheless Coolidge is compelled to add a qualifying statement to this thesis:

> The play is also notable for giving rise to a persistent impression among audiences and critics that the poet's real sympathies are at odds with the ostensible message of the piece.[27]

This element of ambivalence is the basis for the polarization of *Merchant of Venice* criticism into two contrary positions, each representing antithetical extremes of the Christian/Jewish paradigm. At one end of the spectrum of critical opinion, critics take the play at face value as a celebration of Christian love and mercy, with Shylock as a more or less traditional comic villain. At the other end of the critical spectrum, critics see in the play a deep strain of irony that parodies Christian ideals, with Shylock as a more sympathetic character. Sir Frank Kermode represents the first of these perspectives. In an often-quoted essay, he says:

> *The Merchant of Venice*, then is 'about' judgment, redemption and mercy; the supersession in human history of the grim four thousand years of unalleviated justice by the era of love and mercy. It begins with usury and corrupt love. And all the time it tells its audience that this is its subject; only by a determined effort to avoid the obvious can one mistake the theme of *The Merchant of Venice*.[28]

A.D. Moody, responding directly to Kermode, represents a contrary perspective:

> I have to confess that what seems to me obvious, is that the promised supersession of justice by love and mercy does not come about, and that the end is something of a parody of heavenly harmony and love. The play is about the qualities he [Kermode] mentions, but it treats them much more critically than he suggests. He seems to have overlooked the irony that is at the centre of its meaning.
>   To emphasise the importance and centrality of the irony, I would suggest that the play is "about" the manner in which the Christians succeed in the world by not practising their ideals of love and mercy; that it is about their exploitation of an assumed unworldliness to gain the worldly advantage over Shylock; and that, finally, it is about the essential likeness of Shylock and his judges, whose triumph is even more a matter of mercenary justice than his would have been. In this view the play does not celebrate the Christian virtues so much as expose their absence.[29]

In order to justify either one of these contrary poles of opinion, critics have contended that the play is either extremely obvious or extremely ironic. Harley Granville-Barker, for example, sees little in the play that mitigates Shylock's stereotypical villainy: "*The Merchant of Venice* is the simplest of plays, so long as we do not bedevil it with sophistries."[30] In contrast, René Girard is acutely sensitive to nuance and irony:

> Irony is experienced in a flash of complicity with the writer at his most subtle, against the larger and coarser part of the audience that remains blind to those subtleties. Irony is the writer's vicarious revenge against the revenge that he must vicariously perform. If irony were too obvious, if it were intelligible to all, it would defeat its own purpose because there would be no more object for irony to undermine.[31]

It is remarkable that Granville-Barker and Girard could be writing about the same play, yet have such widely divergent views. The contradictions between these antithetical perspectives are difficult to reconcile; likewise the contradictions within each of these perspectives. On one hand, Portia's message of mercy sounds compelling, yet the nominally Christian characters persistently communicate a mixed message in regards to the love that they profess. On the other hand, Shylock attains a level of human dignity that goes beyond the function that he ostensibly serves as a Jew-baiting, anti-Semitic stereotype; yet there is no moral justification for Shylock's vengeful threat to Antonio's life.

One strain in contemporary criticism is more inclined to recognize in the play a fundamental ambiguity that cannot be resolved easily. From this perspective, *The Merchant of Venice* is a paradoxical play that is intended to blend a sense of spiritual dissonance with an ostensible message of divine harmony.[32] As Professor Keith Geary notes:

> All the main characters in the play have double selves, and so sustain apparently contradictory critical readings, one predominating, then the other, making our responses and judgments difficult, shifting, relative. This Janus-like duality is built into the larger design of the play. *The Merchant of Venice* contains a number of 'tricks'—elements that appear to mean one thing but turn out to mean another or, more exactly to have two meanings.[33]

This perspective recognizes that ambiguity *per se* is significant to the play's meaning. However, despite this promising insight, no interpretation has gone beyond the limits of the Christian/Jewish interpretive paradigm.[34] And no interpretation has transcended the thematic dichotomies that derive from the Christian/Jewish interpretive paradigm—mercy versus revenge, love versus hate, generosity versus greed, and the like.

The first 200 years of *Merchant of Venice* interpretation were decidedly unsympathetic to Shylock, the Jew. In the second 200 years of *Merchant* interpretation, sympathy for Shylock began to gain ground as some critics took note of the discrepancy between Christian ideal and Christian behavior in the play. Now that we are beginning the third 200 years of *Merchant of Venice* interpretation, it is time for a revaluation of the play.[35] There is no doubt that Christian/Jewish issues are basic to the meaning of *The Merchant of Venice*, but despite the authority of past precedent it is impossible to grasp the full meaning of this work without reframing the play into a broader context that accommodates the pagan Greco-Roman roots of Western culture as well as the cultural influence of Christianity.

Part one

The subtext of ancient Roman honor

At approximately the mid-point of the play, Bassanio tells Portia that his best friend, Antonio, the merchant of Venice, is the country's foremost personification of ancient Roman honor. He makes this statement when his credibility with her is at its peak. Bassanio has just completed his poetic speech, "So may the outward shows be least themselves," explaining that he is not impressed with superficial appearances (3.2.73-107). He has represented himself to be a sincere and honest individual who stands opposed to deception. And his self-professed integrity seems to have been validated by the test of the three caskets. Like Horatio in the final scene of *Hamlet* who simply says "I am more an antique Roman than a Dane./ Here's yet some liquor left" (*Ham.*, V.ii.325-327), Bassanio speaks of "ancient Roman honour" in a matter-of-fact way that presumes its meaning is self-evident. Bassanio says Antonio is:

> The dearest friend to me, the kindest man,
> The best-conditioned and unwearied spirit
> In doing courtesies, and one in whom
> The ancient Roman honour more appears
> Than any that draws breath in Italy.   (3.2.290-294)

For Bassanio, "ancient Roman honour" is short-hand that describes—more concisely and accurately than a lengthy explanation could—his conception of Antonio's character and integrity.[36]

Shylock might hate Antonio as much as Bassanio loves him, but like Bassanio, he also describes Antonio in terms defined by ancient Rome. When Shylock sees Antonio for the first time early in the play, he fumes to himself: "How like a fawning publican he looks" (1.3.38). A "publican" was one of the ancient Roman Empire's petty bureaucrats, a collector of public taxes or tolls—in other words, someone whose stature was quite a few rungs below the aristocrats who were the exemplars of ancient Roman honor: men of wealth, power and prestige—senators, generals, civic leaders. The word "publican" never appears in the Old Testament (which is pre-Roman), but it is used 24 times in the New Testament, where it is frequently used as a derogatory reference: "Many publicans and sinners came and sat down with him ... And when the Pharisees saw it, they said ... Why eateth your master with publicans and sinners?" (Matt. 9:10-11)[37]. Jesus himself uses "publican" in this derogatory way, as he does when he tells his disciples: "if he [thy brother] neglect to hear the church, let him be unto thee as a heathen man and a publican" (Matt. 18:17). Elsewhere, Jesus says: "I say unto you, That the publicans and the harlots go into the kingdom of God before you" (Matt. 21:31). In using the word "publican," Shylock speaks more like a Christian than a medieval Jew, who most likely would not have been well-versed in the New Testament. Yet Shakespeare did not use "publican" casually, since Shylock's remark is the only instance in which the word is used in all of Shakespeare's work. Shakespeare presumably makes this allusion to ancient Rome with specific artistic intent, even though what that intent might be is not apparent in the context of a Christian/Jewish interpretive paradigm.[37]

In addition to the ancient Roman context that both Shylock and Bassanio rely upon in describing Antonio, the name "Antonio" itself has ancient Roman origins. "Antonio" is a modern variant of the family name of Marcus Antonius (Marc Antony), who traced his patronym back to a son of Hercules called Anton, according to Plutarch's "The Life of Antonius."[39] The common identity (to Shakespeare, at least) of the name "Antonio" with "Antony" or "Antonius" is evident in the First Folio edition of Shakespeare's plays, in which both Julius Caesar and Cleopatra several times call Antony by the more familiar name, "Antonio."[40]

The name "Bassanio" could be related to the ancient Roman "Bassianus," the name given to the son of the Emperor of Rome and brother to the sitting emperor in Shakespeare's *Titus Andronicus*. But more significantly, "Portia"—whose legal ruling determines whether Antonio will live or die—takes her name from one of the true exemplars of ancient Roman honor. The "Portia" of Roman history was Cato's daughter, born into the elite of Roman aristocracy and married to Brutus, who was eulogized by Marc Antony as "the noblest Roman of them all" (*JC*, V.v.ii). Shakespeare ascribed to Portia a degree of nobility that impresses even Brutus, who is inspired and motivated by her to fulfill his destiny as the most noble Roman: "Oh ye gods!," Brutus says. "Render me worthy of this noble wife!" (*JC*, II.i.302-3). Shakespeare explicitly links "Portia" in *The Merchant of Venice* to her ancient Roman namesake. "Her name is Portia, nothing undervalued / To Cato's daughter, Brutus' Portia," Bassanio says to Antonio (1.1.165-166).

As noble wife to the noblest Roman of them all, "Portia" might be expected to judge Antonio according to ancient Roman values, especially since her only previous impression of Antonio is Bassanio's ostensibly credible statement that he is the "one in whom / The ancient Roman honor more appears / Than any that draws breath in Italy" (3.2.292-294). In the scene that determines Antonio's fate, Portia arrives disguised as a young man. She brings a bogus letter of introduction that describes her as "a young doctor of Rome" (4.1.152), presumably an expert in Roman law. She says:

> ...prepare thee to cut off the flesh.
> Shed thou no blood, nor cut thou less nor more
> But just a pound of flesh. If thou tak'st more
> Or less than a just pound, be it so much
> As makes it light or heavy in the substance
> Or the division of the twentieth part

Of one poor scruple— nay, if the scale do turn
But in the estimation of a hair,
Thou diest, and all thy goods are confiscate.   (4.1.320-28)

According to Portia's interpretation of the law, justice hinges upon "the twentieth part of one poor scruple"—that is, upon one twentieth of an ancient Roman unit of measure equivalent to one twenty-fourth of an ounce. In other words, this young doctor of Rome will weigh the scales of justice according to an ancient Roman standard of measure.

In point of fact, ancient Roman law allowed creditors to cut portions of flesh from the bodies of those who defaulted on debts. The Twelve Tables, considered to be a cornerstone of modern Western jurisprudence, formalized rules of honor observed for several hundred years by the patricians of ancient Rome. In this legal code, failure to repay a debt was apparently a capital crime; creditors, it would seem, were permitted to cut shares from the body of the person who was unable to repay what he owed.[41] However, the famous passage on debtor's law in The Twelve Tables of Rome states specifically that a precise and exact measurement of the amount of flesh to be cut is not legally relevant. The Twelve Tables says that "If they [the creditors] have cut more or less than their shares it shall be without prejudice" (Table III, "The Execution of Judgment").[42]

The practice of cutting flesh from the body of the debtor was not uncommon in ancient legal codes, which had detailed rules that stated precisely how much flesh the creditor could cut off, according to Friedrich Nietzsche in *Toward a Genealogy of Morals*. But Nietzsche contended that The Twelve Tables represented "an advance, as evidence of a freer, more generous, more Roman conception of law" because it "decreed it a matter of indifference how much or how little the creditor cut off in such cases: *'si plus minusve secuerunt, ne fraude esto'* (If they have secured more or less, let that be no crime)."[43] The legal rationale that Portia uses to turn the tables (so to speak) against Shylock—that justice hinges upon the variance of "one poor scruple" and that the creditor may take flesh, but no blood—is therefore exactly contrary to Roman law.

The judgment scene in act four is the only scene in which the play's major protagonists—Shylock and Antonio, Portia and Bassanio—meet together, face-to-face. It is the vortex that draws together the play's two most important plot streams— the Antonio/Shylock conflict and the Bassanio/Portia romance. It is the decisive moment that defines the play's spirit. Yet despite the undoubted importance of this scene to the play's structure and meaning, traditional interpretation has not found any particular significance in the fact that this crucial turning point in the play is based upon a festive inversion of ancient Roman law.

Shakespeare scholars have long recognized The Twelve Tables of Rome as a possible source for *The Merchant of Venice*, but they have interpreted Shylock's insistence upon a pound of flesh in terms of the Old Testament's supposedly "eye-for-an-eye" vengefulness rather than as an aspect of Roman law.[44] Shylock is no doubt a Jewish character, but the law that Portia festively inverts is Roman, not Jewish.[45] This apparent contradiction between obvious foreground (Jewish stereotype) and subtle background (ancient Roman law) has no explanation within the Christian/Jewish interpretive paradigm, which fails to find any meaning in Portia's momentous festive inversion of Roman law.

Plautus and Portia

The Merchant of Venice should not be interpreted as if it were a treatise on Christian morality, Elizabethan anti-Semitism or Venetian debtor's law, much less as an essay on ancient Roman honor. This approach ultimately trivializes a work of dramatic art by reducing it to an exposition of concepts drawn from sources external to the play itself. In *A Natural Perspective*, Northrop Frye's book on Shakespearean comedy and romance, Frye says:

> We still talk about Shakespeare's acceptance of legitimacy, divine right, order and degree, the chain of being, Christian eschatology, and the like, as though they were truths that he believed in and wrote his plays to illustrate, or at least did illustrate incidentally. But it seems a strange critical procedure to equate so skillful a dramatic use of a theme with a belief in it which was mere commonplace in his own day and is mere superstition in ours.[46]

A play should be interpreted on its own terms as much as possible, within a context for interpretation defined by the form, content and tradition of its genre. To do otherwise forces a play into a Procrustean bed of ideas that distorts its meaning as a work of dramatic art. "The issue is reduction and how best to avoid it," Professor Harold Bloom writes:

> Rhetorical, Aristotelian, phenomenological and structuralist criticisms all reduce, whether to images, ideas, given things, or phonemes. Moral and other blatant philosophical or psychological criticisms all reduce to rival conceptualizations.[47]

Bloom and Frye agree that the play itself (or poem, as the case may be) must be primary, to be understood only in self-referential terms or in reference to related works of art. "We reduce—if at all—to another poem," Bloom writes.

> The meaning of a poem can only be another poem. This is not a tautology, not even a deep tautology, since the two poems are not the same poem, any more than two lives can be the same life.[48]

Frye pointedly argues against the tendency to reduce the meaning of a play to a moral that could be considered its "real meaning," as if a Shakespeare play were a fable.[49] In these terms, *The Merchant of Venice* would be little more than an exposition of platitudes: love triumphs over hate, good over evil, mercy over revenge and so on. Frye says:

> This quasi-Platonic approach will not work with Shakespeare: his plays are existential facts, and no understanding of them can incorporate their existence. Shakespeare's "meaning" or poetic thought can be expounded only through a structural analysis of the play which keeps the genre of the play in mind as an essential part of the critical context.[50]

With the importance of genre as a first premise, then, it is significant that the literature of Roman comedy was the most dominant contributing factor to the development of comic drama in the Renaissance (and afterward). Roman comedy supplied the fundamental formula that virtually all subsequent comedy employed. It was the model that defined the genre. "At the core of most Renaissance comedy, including Shakespeare's, is the formula transmitted by the New Comedy of Plautus and Terence," according to Frye.[51]

Plautus and Terence were a basic part of the educational curriculum in Shakespeare's day. "While still in the lower school the boys were introduced to Terence and possibly Plautus: Shakespeare's first acquaintance with classical drama, which provided the models of and the inspiration for his first comedies."[52] Students learned Latin language and literature by reading and performing Roman comedies.[53] "Plays were an important part of education both at school and at university, and these were again mainly in Latin," according to Rowse.[54]

This influence may be inferred from the First Folio edition of Shakespeare's work, which designates the various acts and scenes within each play in Latin: *actus primus, actus secundus, actus tertius* and so on, including *scena prima, scena secunda, scena tertia* and so on; the Latin words "exit" or "exeunt" designate when characters are to leave the stage. Shakespearean drama's Latin heritage is evident even today in the common practice of using Roman numerals to cite a specific line, scene or act in a Shakespeare play.

As many know, *The Comedy of Errors* was based on two of Plautus' plays, *The Menoechmi* and *Amphitruo*. But the Plautean model:

> was far more influential than can be indicated by ... any list of direct imitations or borrowings .... For the Elizabethans, it [the Plautean model] offered a standard of comedy, and its plots, persons, and devices were freely used in all kinds of plays, romantic as well as realistic, sentimental as well as satirical or farcical.[55]

Roman comedy, according to Professor Erich Segal, was written for and performed on Roman festival holidays, which provided socially approved relief from Rome's restrictive moral and social codes by:

> turning every day attitudes and everyday values completely upside down. To a society with a fantastic compulsion for hierarchies, order, and obedience, he [Plautus] presents a saturnalian chaos. To a people who regarded a parent's authority with religious awe and could punish any infringement with death, Plautus presents an audacious irreverence for all elders. The atmosphere of his comedy is like that of the medieval Feast of Fools ... which some see as 'providing a safety valve for repressed sentiments which otherwise might have broken their bonds more violently.'[56]

The Roman holidays were occasions for *licentia* and *libertas* [license and liberty], "when the customary restraints of law and morality are thrown aside [for] extravagant mirth and jollity."[57] Part of the appeal Plautus had for his audience is the "fascination which flouting the rules would have had for people so bound by them in everyday life."[58]

The fundamental irony of Roman comedy is based upon the festive inversion of normative morality, an inversion defined in terms of extreme opposites: gross immorality prevails over the strictest honor, deceptive slaves over honest masters, reckless spending over prudent thrift, prodigal sons over restrictive fathers—a reversal of the ordinary moral order. A slave's short speech at the beginning of Plautus' *The Haunted House* summarizes the festive premises of Roman comedy:

So long as you enjoy it so much and can get away with it, go right ahead—have your parties, run through the money, ruin the old man and that fine young son of his. Drink 24 hours a day, live like a bunch of Greeks, buy yourselves mistresses and set them free, feed the scroungers, live off the fat of the land. I suppose these were the orders the old man left when he went abroad [three years ago]? ... Before this, there wasn't a boy in all Athens more concerned about his money or his morals. Now he's running a record for exactly the reverse—thanks to you [a slave] and the education you're giving him.[58]

Parental authority, money and morals are clearly in conflict with the party life, carelessness about preserving and increasing wealth and the bad influence of certain slaves. Festive comedy gives free rein to "exactly the reverse" (as Plautus' character, quoted above, had said) of normative moral values and social expectations. The Saturnalian practice of masters trading places with slaves is representative of this subversive spirit.[60]

Plautus' plays are full of references to religion and morality. Plautus contains:

a great many religious allusions and innumerable references to various deities. This practice contrasts sharply with the style of Terence .... As John Hanson remarks, 'Plautus impresses the student of Roman religion with the sheer quantity of material which he presents. No other Latin author, with the possible exception of St. Augustine, can match him in this respect.'[61]

In contradistinction to Terence, who for the most part refrains from mentioning the gods by name, "Plautine characters do not stop at indirect heresy; they blaspheme the gods themselves."[62] Plautus' festive purpose, according to Segal, was to attack:

the very foundation of Roman morality ... in word and deed .... Sacred practices are parodied with devilish accuracy calculated to remind the audience that ritual is being deliberately stood on its head .... Nothing is sacred in the world of Plautus; irreverence is endemic.[63]

The Romans could easily recognize how comedy inverted normative values; frequent references to religion do not make a comedy a religious work. This irony was so grossly obvious that it did not require extensive elaboration.

The Merchant of Venice is far more subtle in its irony, but has more in common with Roman comedy than with religious literature, despite its many theological references. *The Merchant of Venice* plays upon the fundamental premise of Roman comedy, which is a festive inversion of moral and social values epitomized by the ideal of ancient Roman honor. The context of the genre—comic drama, which is inextricably linked to Roman comedy—defines a festive context for the legal judgment against Shylock. Shakespeare sets up the judgment scene with a festive pretext: Portia tells a lie, claiming that she will devote herself to religious contemplation, when in fact she has a deceptive purpose in mind. She tells "Lorenzo that she will live in a monastery awaiting her husband's return, when in truth she goes to Venice."[64] Shakespeare further reinforces the festive context of the judgment against Shylock when he assigns the interpretation of the law to a character who is a woman masquerading as a man. This so-called "young doctor of Rome" (4.1.152) has "turned o'er many books" (4.1.154-155), which means not only turning over pages to read them, but also overturning the books themselves in the sense of inverting both the letter and spirit of Roman law. In the legal opinion that deflects Shylock's claim to Antonio's flesh, Portia turns Roman law on its head, following the pattern of festive irony typical of Roman comedy.

The cutting of flesh was characteristic of Roman jurisprudence, not a consequence of the plaintiff's personal cruelty or vengefulness. According to Roman law, Shylock's claim to a pound of flesh would have been considered fully justified and morally correct, and mercy for Antonio would have been entirely out of the question. Modern audiences consider carving a pound of human flesh to be a harsh, unfair penalty for a non-performing loan. This contemporary attitude reflects ancient Roman comedy's position on Roman law: it is comedy's festive function to denigrate the law and celebrate the antics of lawbreakers: to portray the law as cruel and unreasonable, as an obstruction to the happiness of good people. Mercy takes precedence over cruel justice in Roman comedy precisely because it is the function of a festival day to subvert the law by forgiving licentiousness, irresponsibility and insubordination. Mercy—for slaves, prodigals and law breakers who might otherwise be executed—is the ultimate irony in Roman comedy. But mercy in this context is the festive validation of Roman immorality, not Christian mercy based on a sublime vision of morality.

In the context of Roman comedy, mercy is not an absolute value, good for its own sake. Instead, it is a pragmatic tactic employed by characters in pursuit of a self-serving end. That's why Portia, who speaks so eloquently about mercy, shortly afterward punishes Shylock by confiscating his money and forcing him to convert to Christianity. Revenge upon the authority figure is no less a function of Roman comedy than mercy for the miscreants. This point is lost upon those who expect to find a genuine example of Christian morality in a Roman-style comedy, such as (for example) Professor Harold C. Goddard, who criticizes Portia's lack of mercy for Shylock as a moral lapse on her part, as a "failure to be true to her inner self."[65]

> Will she show to her victim that quality which at her own divine moment she told us 'is an attribute of God himself'?... Will Portia forget her doctrine that mercy is mercy precisely because it is not deserved?... Will she remember that our prayers for mercy should teach us to do the deeds of mercy and that in the course of justice none of us will see salvation? Alas! She will forget, she will not remember.[66]

Indeed Portia *could* have been a sterling example of glorious

mercy in the manner that Goddard had hoped for, but instead
she gives Shylock a taste of his own medicine. Her course of
action is perfect as a comic reversal, despite Goddard's complaint that it falls short as a gesture of mercy from one who
just a short time previously had said that mercy "is twice blest: /
It blesseth him that gives and him that takes" (4.1.183-184).
But it's irrelevant to criticize Portia for failing to live up to an
ideal of Christian morality that is fundamentally alien to festive comedy. Portia's dramatic purpose in a festive comedy is
to obliterate the prerogatives of lawful authority and conventional morality. Sympathetic treatment for Shylock might have
been consistent with the spirit of compassion that Portia had
preached, but it would have contradicted the logic of comedy,
which allocates mercy to the merrymakers and misery to the
killjoys.

Shakespeare pointedly introduces Portia into the play as a
frivolous personality who does not practice what she preaches.
She is far from being the moral paragon that she is sometimes
expected to be. "It is a good divine that follows his own in-
structions. I can easier teach twenty what were good to be
done, than be one of the twenty to follow mine own teaching,"
Portia says,[68] explaining:

> The brain may devise laws for the blood, but a hot temper leaps o'er
> a cold decree: such a hare is madness, the youth, to skip o'er the
> meshes of good counsel, the cripple.   (1.2.14-20)

Goddard says of the quotation above: "If that is not a specific
preparation for the speech on mercy and what follows it, what
in the name of coincidence is it?"[69] From Goddard's point of
view, though, there is no explanation for Portia's eventual failure to show mercy; he criticizes her "failure to be true to her
inner self"[70] as if she were a real person who actually had an
inner self. Goddard calls Portia "the celestial visitant—the
Portia God made—sent expressly to exorcise the demonic pow-

ers that possess him [Shylock]."[71] But why would Shakespeare introduce Portia into the play as a hot blooded person inclined to behave imprudently if it were his intention that this character should be perceived later in the play as a "celestial visitant," a noble advocate for lofty ideals? If it is Portia's dramatic purpose to teach the world a lesson in divine mercy, then why does she so promptly fall short of the ideal that she preaches? And why does this "celestial visitant" lie about going to a monastery as a prelude to delivering a supposedly religious message?

Some critics (Kermode, for example) assert that it is self-evident that Portia's dramatic function is to represent the ideal of Christian mercy. But this hypothesis cannot be justified without some fairly convoluted reasoning: first, Portia is introduced as "hot-blooded" and frivolous; then she lies and disguises herself as a man. She is then suddenly transfigured into a personification of lofty and sublime ideals—only to promptly revert back to a flawed moral state, in which she compromises the ideal that she had briefly espoused. She then spends the remainder of the play engaging in bawdy dialogue about her husband's presumed infidelity. Far from defining her dramatic purpose, Portia's brief interlude as a supposed moral pontificator seems to contradict what we know of her from elsewhere in the play.

A character who preaches Christian morality does not fit in well with what we know about the morality of festive comedy. Rather that trying to define Portia's dramatic role on the basis of assumptions that contradict everything we know about her, it is a far simpler to perceive Portia as a festive/frivolous personality whose behavior remains consistent throughout the play. Portia is not miraculously transformed into a saint for one speech only; her speech on mercy is a bit of moral flim-flammery that is consistent with her dramatic function in a Plautine-style comedy, which celebrates festive immorality.

Interpretations of *The Merchant of Venice* that find a spiritual ideal (rather than comic irony) in Portia's famous plea for mercy misread the moral tone of comedy, which ridiculed decency and morality. A serious moral statement, intended by the author to be taken at face value, would be out of place in this context, as would any character who is presumed to speak as a shining beacon of sincerity and truth. There is no place in a Roman-style comedy for a genuine example of moral decency. On the contrary, it would be typical of a Roman-style comedy for a self-serving character to deliver an ironic send-up of society's moral pieties; and the more "noble" this character sounds in doing so, the better.

Debt and desire

The ancient Romans greatly valued prudence and self-restraint in regard to money as well as morality. "Sound investment policy... was in fact considered a Roman virtue," according to Segal.

> It is well attested that the Romans were extremely fond of money and would pass up no opportunity for financial gain. Horace's picture of the Roman father teaching his son to enlarge his patrimony serves well to describe Cato the Elder, who, according to Plutarch, considered a man who increased the capital he inherited to be 'marvelous and godlike'...."[72]

Although thriftiness and financial self-interest are said by some to be Jewish character traits, the more salient point is that these qualities are elemental to the ethos of Roman honor. In contrast, the typical character in Roman comedy is impulsive and imprudent, squanders his money and pursues romantic entanglements with the wrong sort of girl. Consequently, Segal states that "the most common dilemma presented in Plautine comedy is that of a young man *amens et egens*, in love and insolvent...."[73]

Bassanio fits this description precisely. He has gone broke

pursuing romantic ventures. He owes a great deal of money to Antonio as a consequence of flaunting—and squandering—the trappings of borrowed wealth. "'Tis not unknown to you," Bassanio says to Antonio,

> How much I have disabled mine estate
> By something showing a more swelling port
> Than my faint means would grant continuance....
> ... my chief care
> Is to come fairly off from the great debts
> Wherein my time something too prodigal
> Hath left me gaged. (1.1.122-130)

Bassanio seems to be speaking frankly and sincerely when he says that his "chief care," his primary concern, is paying off his debts. Romantic considerations don't seem to be an issue. Bassanio proposes to recoup his financial losses by pursuing the same course of action that got him into debt in the first place. He proposes to show a "swelling port" once more; this time he hopes it will pay off:

> In my schooldays, when I had lost one shaft,
> I shot his fellow the selfsame flight
> The selfsame way with more advised watch
> To find the other forth, and by adventuring both
> I oft found both. I urge this childhood proof
> Because what follows is pure innocence.
> I owe you much; and, like a wilful youth,
> That which I owe is lost; but if you please
> To shoot another arrow that self way
> Which you did shoot the first, I do not doubt,
> As I will watch the aim, or to find both
> Or bring your latter hazard back again
> And thankfully rest debtor for the first. (1.1.140-152)

Bassanio positions his romantic prospects with Portia as a type of gamble that might enable him to recoup financial losses incurred from previous gambles. With Antonio's financial backing, then, Bassanio will have "the means/ To hold a rival place" (1.1.173-4) among Portia's suitors. He is hopeful that he can marry Portia, and then repay (with Portia's money) debts accumulated from his previous romantic ventures: "I have a mind presages me such thrift/ That I should questionless be fortunate" (1.1.175-176). His choice of words—"thrift" and "fortunate"—leave no doubt that although he later selects the casket of lead, he has a very definite interest in Portia's gold.[74] Speaking to his closest friend, Bassanio describes Portia as "a lady richly left" (1.1.161)—in other words, a wealthy heiress. "Nor is the wide world ignorant of her worth" (1.1.167), he says in an ambiguous reference that alludes to Portia's wealth as well as to her other qualities.

Bassanio speaks of Portia as a "golden fleece" (1.1.170), noting that "many Jasons come in quest of her" (1.1.172)—a double reference both to Portia's blond hair and her immense wealth, reflecting the duality of Bassanio's situation: he is both in love and in debt. "The golden fleece was a symbol of the fortunes for which merchants ventured," according to John R. Brown, who cites several examples of this usage in Elizabethan literature.[75] "This figurative gold involves matters of real gold, 3,000 ducats," observes Professor Philip Edwards:

> Bassanio says frankly that winning the rich Portia will be the means of getting clear of his heavy debts. To set himself up as a suitor is going to cost money which he hasn't got, and hence his application to Antonio for funds, and hence Antonio's application to Shylock. Down to the waist *The Merchant of Venice* is romance; beneath all realism, or to change the image, the flower of romance is rooted in a heavy clay of sordid pecuniary needs and their consequence.[76]

In speaking of Portia as a "golden fleece," Bassanio identifies himself with ancient Roman literary tradition generally, but more specifically with Jason, who was notoriously insincere—that is to say, dishonest and manipulative—in the way in which he betrayed Medea after taking advantage of her love in order to achieve his own ambition. (The insincerity of Bassanio's promise never to remove his fidelity ring is exposed in act five.)

Bassanio's monetary interest in Portia is not something trivial to be glossed over; it is pivotal to the structure of the play as the *causa sine qua non* of both the Bassanio/Portia romance and the Antonio/Shylock conflict. Bassanio's need for money is the reason for his courtship of Portia, which in turn becomes the reason for Antonio's debt to Shylock. The money borrowed from Shylock provides Bassanio with the financial backing he needs to court Portia. The fundamental importance to the structure of the play of Bassanio's need for money is beyond question. The issue is: what is its relevance to the play's meaning?

Hypothetically, the reasons for Bassanio's debt to Antonio could have been noble, rather than frivolous. For example, he could have gone broke because he had been supporting a sickly mother and 12 siblings. But instead, he's lost Antonio's money in a variety of romantic escapades that have failed to pay off— a circumstance that does not make him evil, but which cannot be justified credibly with an idealistic rationale. If we assume that Bassanio, like Portia, is supposed to represent some sort of idealized romantic hero (to be contrasted with Shylock's greedy materialism), then why does Shakespeare initially define Bassanio's personality with the unsavory characteristics of a frivolous, debt-ridden gold digger? Antonio's debt to Shylock is the sore thumb that sticks out to remind us that Bassanio is something less than the dignified, self-sufficient man of honor who would be highly desirable to a woman of wealth and position. Bassanio's consistent pattern of imprudent behavior and his mercenary interest in Portia contradict the notion that he could be a noble fellow who sincerely loves Portia for her finer qualities alone.

When *The Merchant of Venice* is interpreted from within the confines of a Christian/Jewish interpretive paradigm, there is presumed to be a conflict between "Christian" positives (idealism, integrity, love) and "Jewish" negatives (materialism, greed, revenge). In this context, Bassanio's prodigality, debts and mercenary intent serve no dramatic purpose; neither does his subsequent deceit with the wedding ring, which has no bearing on Christian/Jewish conflict *per se*. Bassanio's spiritual shortcomings, though manifestly evident, have no meaning within the Christian/Jewish paradigm. However, Bassanio's character flaws make perfect sense within the context of a comedy in the Plautine mode, in which his financial interest in Portia doesn't invalidate the purity of his romantic intentions because no purity on his part is assumed. On the contrary, his quest for both love and money defines him as a frivolous, ignoble character in the style of the Plautine prototype.

Broken promises of love

Making promises—but not keeping them—is a major part of courtship style in *The Merchant of Venice*. Jessica says of Lorenzo that he "did ... swear he loved her well, / Stealing her soul with many vows of faith, / And ne'er a true one" (5.1.19-20). Graziano describes his courtship of Nerissa as "swearing till my very roof was dry / With oaths of love, at last, if promise last, / I got a promise of this fair one here" (3.2.204-206). "And do you, Graziano, mean good faith?" Bassanio asks (3.2.210). "Yes, faith, my lord," Graziano replies (3.2.211). Of course, he later demonstrates bad faith in several ways.

A major portion of act five emphasizes to Bassanio and Graziano the importance of a personal promise. This focus in the concluding act of the play reinforces the significance of the issue of honor—honesty and integrity—to the meaning of the play. Like Portia, Nerissa had also made her husband swear that he would never part with his wedding ring (4.2.14). Graziano swears that he has kept his word. However, he does so within a context of festive irony dominated by the moon, in which the truth and falsehood are inverted: "By yonder moon I swear you do me wrong" (5.1.142), Graziano says. By ordinary light, he has broken his promise. But with shimmering, illusory moonlight as his moral benchmark, he claims that he has remained true to his word.[77]

Overhearing this argument, Portia says, "A quarrel, ho, already! What's the matter?" (5.1.146) Graziano replies that the disagreement is:

> About a hoop of gold, a paltry ring
> That she did give me, whose posy was
> For all the world like cutler's poetry
> Upon a knife—'Love me, and leave me not.'   (5.1.147-150)

The ring was important to him when he promised never to remove it, but it is a paltry hoop of gold when he is discovered without it. Graziano's broken promise is typical behavior for a character in a Roman-style comedy; it is the festive inverse of the fidelity to an oath that ancient Roman honor would have demanded. His reference to "cutler's poetry/ Upon a knife" associates the promise of fidelity with the cutting of flesh, which echoes Portia's self-mutilation with a knife to prove (in *Julius Caesar*, II.i.292-302) that she has the resolve to remain true to her word. It also echoes the knife that would be used to cut flesh in enforcement of Shylock's bond, as well as the knives that would have enforced the debtor's law in The Twelve Tables of Rome. Yet Graziano mentions "cutler's poetry" in order to trivialize both the ring and the sentiment of its inscription (a longing for faithfulness).

Nerissa does not accept arguments that would belittle the ring's importance. She focuses clearly on what the ring represents: the promise of fidelity. And she is very clear that Graziano has broken that promise, which he previously had claimed was not at all trivial.

> You swore to me when I did give it you
> That you would wear it till your hour of death,
> And that it should lie with you in your grave.
> Though not for me, yet for your vehement oaths

You should have been respective and have kept it.   (5.1.152-156)

This discussion sets up a similar confrontation between Portia and Bassanio. "I gave my love a ring," Portia says:

... and made him swear
Never to part with it; and here he stands.
I dare be sworn for him he would not leave it,
Nor pluck it from his finger, for the wealth
That the world masters. Now, in faith, Graziano
You give your wife too unkind a cause of grief,
And 'twere to me, I should be mad at it.   (5.1.170-176)

The issue here is the promise of fidelity—keeping a promise such that a man's word is his bond. The words "swear," "sworn," and "faith" are repeated often. At this point in the play, Bassanio begins to understand what his wife expects of him in terms of trustworthiness and fidelity: "Why I were best to cut my left hand off,/ And swear that I lost the ring defending it" (5.1.177-178), he mutters under his breath. Of course, if he were to take that drastic action and make that claim, he would be telling yet another lie. However, in this hypothetical deception of last resort, Bassanio finally comprehends that keeping a personal promise should be guaranteed by flesh and blood, in the manner similar to Portia's conception of ancient Roman honor in *Julius Caesar*, which we will examine more closely later.

Knowing full well that Bassanio has given his ring away, Portia says she believes he wouldn't "pluck" the ring "from his finger for the wealth/ That the world masters." When Bassanio admits that the ring is gone, Portia says: "Even so void is your false heart of truth" (5.1.189). This rebuke is an unequivocal message, even though it is delivered in the play-ful spirit of comic irony. Portia hammers home to Bassanio the importance of fidelity to a promise, specifically faulting him for his failure of honor:

> If you had known the virtue of the ring,
> Or half her worthiness that gave the ring,
> Or your own honour to contain the ring,
> You would not then have parted with the ring:
> What man is there so much unreasonable,
> If you had pleased to have defended it
> With any terms of zeal, wanted the modesty
> To urge the thing held as a ceremony?
> Nerissa teaches me what to believe:
> I'll die for't, but some woman had the ring!   (5.1.199-208)

Portia knows that "some woman" has the ring because in fact she is the woman who has the ring in her possession. "No, by my honour, madam," Bassanio replies. "By my soul / No woman had it" (5.1.209-210), he asserts, not knowing, as Portia does, that he certainly did give the ring to a woman. Bassanio claims it was his honor that compelled him to give the ring away: "My honour would not let ingratitude / So much besmear it" (5.1.218-219). But Bassanio's claim to honor is another instance of festive irony; it is the inverse of what honor would be under non-festive circumstances: keeping a promise, not compromising it.

The play comes full circle with Antonio's offer to guarantee Bassanio's promise of fidelity. At the beginning of the play, Antonio guarantees a monetary loan to Bassanio with the flesh of his body (in his bond with Shylock). At the end of the play, he guarantees Bassanio's promise of faithfulness with his own soul:

> I once did lend my body for his wealth
> Which, but for him that had your husband's ring,
> Had quite miscarried. I dare be bound again,
> My soul upon the forfeit, that your lord
> Will never more break faith advisedly.   (5.1.249-253)

In making this offer, Antonio concedes that Bassanio has broken his faith with Portia, an admission that Bassanio himself has just made (5.1.248-249). That Antonio offers himself as surety for Bassanio both at the beginning of the play and at the end—first his body for money, then his soul for fidelity—defines a structural balance that indicates spiritual progress on Bassanio's part. The first time Antonio offers himself as surety for Bassanio he is meeting Bassanio's need for money; he puts his flesh on the line. This gesture confirms by implication that Bassanio was materially-focused at the beginning of the play. The second time that he offers himself as a surety for Bassanio he puts his soul on the line. It is a gesture of an entirely different order, and confirms by implication Antonio's confidence that Bassanio has learned a spiritual lesson by the end of the play. "Then you shall be his surety," Portia replies. "Give him this [the ring], / And bid him keep it better than the other" (5.1.254-255). And of course, by "the other," she means the inverse: "the same"—it is the same ring that she had given him originally.

The play concludes with Bassanio's confession and apology, along with his vow never to break a promise again. "Pardon this fault, and by my soul I swear/ I never more will break an oath with thee" (5.1.247-248). The importance of this lesson is underlined by Graziano, who has the final word in the play, leaving the audience with these words: "Well, while I live, I'll fear no other thing / So sore as keeping safe Nerissa's ring" (5.1.306-307). Together, these two concluding statements affirm that the play is "about" the importance of keeping a promise—which is as important in the romantic world of Belmont as it is in the commercial world of Venice.

The Christian/Jewish interpretive paradigm imposes upon the play themes such as revenge versus mercy, or love versus hate, that give disproportionate thematic weight to Shylock, but have little to do with Bassanio and Portia's romance and therefore little relevance to the final act of the play. "Critics have almost unanimously dismissed the ring episode—and so one-fifth of the play!—as 'but a superficial matter' after the court scene," according to Geary. "This verdict fails to recognize that the ring episode is almost a re-enactment of the trial itself, but focusing this time on the play's second bond, the marriage bond."[78]

In his summary of critical opinion on the play, Professor John Lyon assumes that act five is without a theme because the Christian/Jewish thematic issues were resolved in act four:

> It is a very odd play that gets a new and independent plot fully under way only [in] its last Act. The oddity is compounded by the way in which the ring plot teases us with echoes of what had preceded it, but echoes only half-heard since they seem to resist specificity and pointedness. Events at the end of the play set us thinking about the play's relatedness but withhold the more precise elaborations which might give a fuller substantiality to our speculations....
>
> The tangential ring plot appears to contain, not a development, but a niggling residue of the play's earlier concerns. Underlying its immediate pleasures, there appear to be conflicting intentions at work, none fully and unequivocally realized.[79]

But while the Christian/Jewish paradigm cannot easily integrate act five into themes that give meaning to the entire play, in contrast the honor/irony interpretive paradigm gives all five acts of the play a thematic integrity that, for the most part, is lacking in traditional interpretation. The festive violation of a bond is the common denominator between the play's two major plot streams—the Antonio/Shylock and Bassanio/Portia stories. And the ring as a symbol of fidelity is also common to both plot streams, with Jessica giving away Shylock's ring and Bassanio giving away his own. The issue of a broken bond gives the play an evenly balanced structure and represents the deeper thematic unity that underlies the superficial distinctions of themes typical of the Christian/Jewish interpretive paradigm, themes such as hate versus love, and mercy versus justice, that come to a head in act four with the judgment scene, but do not seem to have much relevance to act five.

The bond between Venice and Belmont

The sanctity of a bond—whether a personal promise, a legal obligation or a marital or family bond—is fundamental to the ideal of ancient Roman honor. The comic inversion of this ideal—the festive violation of a bond—is the unifying theme of *The Merchant of Venice* and a constant throughout the play, whether it be a debtor's bond in Venice, the world of commerce; a marital bond in Belmont, the world of romance; or Jessica's breaking of a family bond, which spans both Venice and Belmont. In business, Antonio fails to keep to the terms of his bond with Shylock. In romance, Bassanio and Graziano break the trust of their marital bonds by wishing that their wives were dead and giving away the rings they promised never to remove. And Jessica, who flees from Venice to Belmont, breaks faith with her family bond by stealing money and giving away her mother's ring.

Marriage integrates opposite extremes—love and legality, romance and property rights, the spiritual and the carnal: issues that are ostensibly antithetical, but equally important in the supposedly antithetical spheres of Belmont and Venice. Wedding vows, symbolized by the wedding ring, include contractual property rights no less than promises of faithful love. When Bassanio selects the casket that wins Portia, she says to him:

> Myself and what is mine to you and yours
> Is now converted. But now I was the lord
> Of this fair mansion, master of my servants,
> Queen o'er myself; and even now, but now,
> This house, these servants, and this same myself
> Are yours, my lord's. I give them with this ring,
> Which when you part from, lose, or give away,
> Let it presage the ruin of your love
> And be my vantage to exclaim on you.   (3.2.166-174)

Clearly the ring is a property contract no less than a promise of love. One would think that Portia's elaboration upon this point, and her stern warning not to give the ring away, would have been sufficiently compelling to preclude any confusion about the ring's importance. Bassanio seems to understand, vowing (in so many words) that this ring will leave his finger only over his dead body. Unlike Antonio, he does not face a possible death sentence in a court of law. But he himself posits that breaking his word would be morally equivalent to a capital crime, in effect equal to the penalty that Antonio might have paid for failing to live up to his bond. "When this ring / Parts from this finger," Bassanio says, "then parts life from hence. / O, then be bold to say Bassanio's dead" (3.2.183-185).

Traditional *Merchant of Venice* criticism usually emphasizes the difference between business relationships and personal relationships in order to more sharply delineate conflicting moral issues. Shylock is supposedly a stingy materialist who sticks to the letter of the law because he is narrow of spirit; Bassanio and Antonio, on the other hand, are supposedly more generous of spirit and are, unlike Shylock, not narrow-minded sticklers for detail. Putting aside, however, the emotional reactions that the Jewish character Shylock can provoke, Bassanio's violation of his vow never to remove Portia's ring is fundamentally identical to Antonio's failure to meet the terms of Shylock's bond. A bond of debt is a formalized promise to pay, subject to legal enforcement. A marital bond is also a formalized promise, with legal standing in a court of law; and Portia had specifically stipulated that there would be significant financial implications associated with Bassanio's promise never to remove the ring: "This house, these servants... are yours...I give them with this ring," (3.2.170-171). Both Bassanio and Antonio fail to deliver on a solemn, personal promise or commitment.

Antonio's default on the terms of his bond with Shylock is ostensibly a more serious matter than Bassanio's violation of faith with Portia. But in non-festive circumstances, Bassanio's broken promises to Portia would be no less serious than Antonio's default on his bond with Shylock; it would disrupt and spoil his relationship with Portia, which would be no laughing matter. It might even prove to be fatally tragic, as it does for Desdemona in *Othello*.

Consider for a moment the similarities between Bassanio's situation in *The Merchant of Venice* and Desdemona's in *Othello*. Bassanio has given away a ring, his "wife's first gift" (5.1.167); and Portia, his wife, confronts him about the absence of this important symbol of their relationship. Similarly, Othello confronts Desdemona about the missing handkerchief, which was his first gift to her and which he asked her never to give away. Emilia, Iago's wife, describes the handkerchief as Desdemona's "first remembrance from the Moor," which Othello "conjur'd her she should ever keep it" (*Oth.*, III.iii.290-296).[80] Bassanio gave his ring away frivolously, while Desdemona had treasured the handkerchief; nevertheless, she does not have the handkerchief available when Othello demands that she show it to him, which Othello construes as proof that she has been unfaithful to him. This proof of infidelity is quite false, but Othello believes that she gave away his first gift to her, which he regards as a breach of honor on her part (*Oth.*, IV.i.14-16). His own honor requires him to rectify this affront by killing her. In contrast, Portia does not merely infer dishonorable behavior from a missing gift; she knows for certain that Bassanio has broken trust with her because she herself had heard him say that he wished that she were dead, just as she later was present in person when he gave away his fidelity ring. However, the result is bawdy teasing when Portia confronts Bassanio about the ring he promised never to give away, not the tragedy that results when Othello infers that Desdemona gave away his first gift to her, breaking her promise never to part with it.

The missing first gift, symbolic of a violation of honor, is the common denominator between the comedy of *The Merchant* and the tragedy of *Othello*. Although the metaphor—a lover's first gift as a promise of fidelity—is common to both plays, its meaning is determined by the paradigm within which it is interpreted. The distorting lens of comedy's festive irony is predisposed to vilify the law and wink at infidelity; in comedy, various travesties are both expected and accepted without any adverse consequence. However, in tragedy there are grave consequences indeed for violations of trust and honor, both in law and in love.

No doubt there are significant differences between Shylock and the other Venetians—differences in appearance, personality, religious belief. However, once again putting aside any reaction to the emotional issues associated with Jewish/Christian conflict, Shylock and the Christians do not represent conflicting ideals. They represent conflicting perspectives on a common ideal, that of ancient Roman honor. Shylock's dramatic function is to represent ancient Roman honor from the non-festive perspective, as the obstacle and antagonist to those who would be merry. The Christians' dramatic function is to represent ancient Roman honor from a festive perspective, which is to say, to subvert and invert that ideal and all that it implies. Money and love—Venice and Belmont—are not antithetical in the context of a Roman-style comedy, which celebrates the happiness that derives from both money and love, while making light of the legal and personal obligations that both money and love might impose.

Flesh, blood and ancient Roman honor

Ancient Roman honor is the *ne plus ultra* of normative self-restraint, the sharpest possible antithesis to festive self-indulgence. It is not a central issue in Plautine comedy; but as the strictest formulation of Roman culture's governing values, it is always festive comedy's implied foil. Comedy plays upon the ironies of mistaken identity in contradistinction to the man of honor who is, for the most part, without irony: he is exactly what he appears to be. He refuses to deceive; he is straightforward, uncomplicated and honest. He says what he means without any dissimulation, declining to manipulate appearances either in jest or for the sake of his self-interest. Above all, he keeps his promises, meets his obligations and tells the truth. For the man of ancient Roman honor, appearance and reality are not separate and variable; they are integral to his being and constant.

These character traits of ancient Roman honor are precisely the qualities that Shakespeare attributed in *Coriolanus* to the noble Caius Marcius (later called Coriolanus). Despite his military heroism, Coriolanus suffers political defeat and death because of his absolute refusal to "dissemble" (*Cor.*, III.iii.62). He does not alter his blunt-speaking personality even though it would be "politically incorrect" (as we would say today) and therefore offensive to the plebeians. "Must I / With my base tongue give to my noble heart / A lie that it must bear?" (*Cor.*, III.iii.99-101), he asks. His lack of diplomatic tact is a reflection of his strong personal commitment to telling the truth as he sees it. One of the first statements Coriolanus makes in the play reveals that telling the truth is a fundamental principle for him: "I'll fight with none but thee, for I do hate thee / Worse than a promise breaker" (I.viii.1-2). In short, he has many of the traits that Aristotle attributes to man of greatness:

> He must also be open in his hate and in his love (for to conceal one's feelings, i.e., to care less for truth than for what people will think, is a coward's part), and must speak and act openly; for he is free of speech because he is contemptuous, and his is given to telling the truth, except when he speaks in irony to the vulgar.[81]

The man of honor doesn't merely "keep" his word. He is a man of his word to the point where he and his word are one.

The man of honor does not merely appear to be honorable; he is honorable to the core of his being, down to the bone, in his flesh and blood—deep down inside, in sharpest possible antithesis to what merely appears to be true at a superficial level. As the "noblest Roman of them all," Brutus thinks of his personal integrity as if it were his flesh and blood, as if his honor were so deeply embedded in his being that it runs in his veins:

> ... every drop of blood
> That every Roman bears, and nobly bears,
> Is guilty of a several bastardy,
> If he do break the smallest particle
> Of any promise that hath pass'd from him.   (*JC*, II.i.136-140)

The identification of blood with honor echoes The Twelve Tables of Rome, which stipulated an equivalence between a man's honor and his flesh and blood.[82]

Brutus stakes "every drop of blood" on the "smallest particle of any promise." In contrast, Portia invokes the smallest possible Roman unit of measurement ("the twentieth part of one poor scruple") when she devises a legal loophole that enables Antonio to escape from the terms of his bond. Portia insists that the terms of Shylock's bond do not entitle him to a single drop of Antonio's blood, while the single drop of blood was the ultimate measure of fidelity to a bond for Brutus. Portia's legal ruling is therefore a mirror image of Brutus' commitment to ancient Roman honor—and like a mirror image, it is exactly opposite to that which it reflects.

Brutus, with his deeply ingrained commitment to honor, deems a formal bond to be relatively superficial and therefore superfluous. Speaking to the other conspirators plotting Caesar's assassination, he asserts that only those who are weak in spirit and lacking in integrity would have need for a bond—not noble Romans who are above any hint of doubt that they will hold fast to their intention. To suggest that a formal oath or bond might reinforce this intention is, in Brutus' opinion, tantamount to suggesting that the noble Roman's personal commitment had been somewhat weak in the first place and had needed to be reinforced—a possibility that Brutus emphatically rejects:

> What need we any spur but our own cause
> To prick us to redress? what other bond
> Than secret Romans, that have spoke the word
> And will not falter? and what other oath
> Than honesty to honesty engag'd
> That this shall be, or we will fall for it?
> Swear priests and cowards and men cautelous,
> Old feeble carrions and such suffering souls
> That welcome wrongs; unto bad causes swear
> Such creatures as men doubt; but do not stain
> The even virtue of our enterprise,
> Nor th' insuppressive mettle of our spirits,
> To think that our cause or our performance
> Did need an oath   (II.i.123-140)

Brutus says that no formal contract is needed to "prick us to redress," using words that suggest cutting and bleeding, similar to the redress that would have been stipulated by The Twelve Tables of Rome in order to rectify a broken bond of debt. These words have their echo in *The Merchant of Venice*, where Shylock responds to Solanio's taunts with a famously angry speech, "If you prick us do we not bleed?" (3.1.60-61).

Solanio, one of Antonio's friends, mocks Shylock, calling him "old carrion" (3.1.33). In speaking of Roman integrity, Brutus contrasts the "insuppressive mettle" of the Roman spirit with "old feeble carrion"—dead meat, meat without blood, the life force; meat that won't bleed when it is cut. Like Brutus, Shylock uses "carrion" as a term of contempt for those who do not keep to the terms of their bonds: "You'll ask me why I rather choose to have / A weight of carrion flesh, than to receive / Three thousand ducats. I'll not answer that" (4.1.39-41). A man without honor is equivalent to carrion, according to this perspective. But while Shylock's use of the word "carrion" is similar to Brutus,' it is opposite to Solanio's. Solanio calls Shylock "carrion" precisely because Shylock wants to hold both Antonio and Jessica to the terms of their bond; and Shylock equates a bond—both a family bond and a debtor's bond—with flesh and blood.

One test of a person's mettle is the ability to remain constant in resolve, even at the cost of physical pain in general and wounds to the flesh and loss of blood in particular. Brutus says:

> ... hollow men, like horses hot at hand,
> Make gallant show and promise of their mettle;
> But when they should endure the bloody spur,
> They fall their crests, and like deceitful jades
> Sink in the trial. (IV.ii.23-27)

Brutus' wife Portia shows her mettle to "endure the bloody spur" when she voluntarily stabs herself in the thigh, revealing to Brutus the cold resolve in her commitment to honor and to their marital bond. She first pleads with Brutus to speak openly "within the bond of marriage" (*JC*, II.i.280), invoking "all your vows of love, and that great vow/ Which did incorporate and make us one" (*JC*, II.i.272-273). Brutus replies: "You are my true and honourable wife, / As dear to me as are the ruddy drops / That visit my sad heart" (*JC*, II.i.288-290). Once again, as he did when speaking with the conspirators, Brutus equates honor with drops of blood.

Portia cites her family relationships—wife of Brutus, daughter of Cato—to support her claim to nobility. She then mutilates herself to prove definitively that she has the steely self-discipline to hold fast to a promise (in this case, to keep secret the brewing conspiracy to assassinate Caesar) and maintain her honor:

> I grant I am a woman; but withal
> A woman that Lord Brutus took to wife.
> I grant I am a woman; but withal

A woman well reputed, Cato's daughter.
Think you I am no stronger than my sex,
Being so fathered and so husbanded?
Tell me your [Brutus'] counsels, I will not disclose 'em.
I have made strong proof of my constancy,
Giving myself a voluntary wound
Here in the thigh; can I bear that with patience,
And not my husband's secrets?   (*JC*, II.i.292-302)[83]

The Twelve Tables of Rome stipulated that flesh should be cut from the body as a penalty for breaking an obligation, but Portia preemptively cuts her own flesh as tangible proof that she *will not* break a commitment. Ancient Roman honor, both for Portia and The Twelve Tables, is backed by flesh and blood. Portia's self-mutilation is the gesture that prompts Brutus' remark: "O ye gods, render me worthy of this noble wife" (II.ii.303-304). He recognizes that cutting flesh is proof positive of ancient Roman honor.[84]

The ring: a vow wedded to flesh and blood

A wedding ring represents fidelity to a vow, fidelity to the bond of marriage. For Portia in *The Merchant of Venice*, no less than for Portia in *Julius Caesar*, these vows are inextricably linked to flesh and blood. The wedding ring symbolizes a marital bond that legally consolidates the property of husband and wife and spiritually unites them into one flesh. The ring represents a point of convergence where affection becomes legally binding, where a personal promise becomes a legal contract, and where personal promise and legal contract are fused with flesh and blood.

In *The Merchant of Venice*, Shakespeare links "wedding ring" to flesh in two ways. First, Shakespeare implicitly links "ring" to flesh when he uses the word "ring" as a bawdy pun that alludes to the physical side of marital relations. It was relatively common in Renaissance literature to use the word "ring" as a way of referring to female genitalia. Graziano therefore can be understood in both a carnal and spiritual sense when he says: "Well, while I live, I'll fear no other thing / So sore as keeping safe Nerissa's ring" (5.1.306-307).[85] The wedding ring and pleasures of the flesh are directly related, as Portia and Nerissa make clear when they accuse their husbands of giving their rings away to other women, and when they later state their intention to share body and bed with the person who possesses the ring (5.1.228).

Second, Shakespeare explicitly links the word "ring" to flesh in a statement of Portia's that stipulates the equivalence of a personal promise to flesh and blood. Portia says that promises of love and fidelity should to be kept as closely as the wedding ring clings to the finger. When there is a strong commitment to the marital bond and marriage vows, the ring should become virtually a part of the body, as Portia makes clear when she rebukes Graziano for giving his ring away:

> You were to blame ...
> To part so slightly with your wife's first gift,
> A thing stuck on with oaths upon your finger
> And so riveted with faith unto your flesh. (5.1.166-69)

Here Portia states definitively her belief that the personal promise should be integrated with flesh and blood—"riveted with faith unto your flesh." She wants more than mere correspondence between what a man says and what he does; she wants an equivalence of man and word, oath and flesh, similar to that which Brutus had postulated.

In the context of festive comedy, it is to be expected that Bassanio and Graziano will break their promises and give away their rings. In the same spirit, Jessica gives away the ring that her mother gave to Shylock, her father. In contrast, Shylock—the authority figure representing non-festive values—treasures the ring that he had received from his late wife prior to their marriage. "Out upon her! Thou torturest me, Tubal," Shylock rages, when he learns that Jessica has escaped from his house, stolen this family keepsake and traded it for a monkey. "It was my turquoise. I had it of Leah when I was a bachelor. I would not have given it for a wilderness of monkeys" (3.1.113-116). Shylock's attachment to this ring stands in stark contrast to the careless frivolity with which Jessica, Graziano and Bassanio give away rings that they should have regarded as deeply meaningful.

Shylock is of course upset that Jessica has taken money and other valuables, but his rage is not motivated solely by monetary loss. Jessica has desecrated the family bond, first of all, by leaving home, and second, by discarding an irreplaceable memento of her late mother, a keepsake that had more than mere monetary value in Shylock's eyes and should have represented something more personal and meaningful than money to her as well. However, Jessica adds insult to injury when she trades this family heirloom for a monkey. This gesture of disrespect for a symbol of her parents' fidelity to each other is a jarring blow of emotional violence, a foolish and insensitive deed that goes far beyond the bounds of the simple, good-humored merriment supposedly characteristic of the play's Christians. "Lorenzo's enterprise in stealing Jessica wins our sympathy partly because it is done in a masque, as a merriment," writes C.L. Barber.[86] But why should trading a treasured family memento for a monkey win our sympathy? What meaning does this gesture have in the presumed context of noble generosity and Christian love? In the context of Roman comedy there is no doubt about the meaning of actions like these. In a festive context, no one would presume that slaves and prodigals were particularly good or noble; on the contrary, they are disrespectful to their parents and spouses. Therefore it would be a mistake to idealize as noble and generous the outrageous comic impropriety typical of characters in a Roman-style comedy. As René Girard notes:

> Those critics who idealize the Venetians write as if the many textual clues that contradict their view were not planted by the author himself, as if their presence in the play were a purely fortuitous matter, like the arrival of a bill in the morning mail, when one really expects a love letter.[87]

Roman comedy can be merry while also having a crude, rude, ugly edge that is socially and morally repugnant—because it is the festival day's function to desecrate conventional moral values by inverting them.

It is Shylock's comic function (as the *idiotes*[88] in this play) to be at war with the all the prodigals' festive values, just as it is the comic function of everyone else to be at war with him. To be sure, Shylock is an anti-Semitic stereotype, but his Jewish identity is secondary to his dramatic function: to be the foil to those comic characters who would subvert the civilized values of thrift, rightful authority, justice and law. This dramatic function is performed in other Shakespeare comedies by non-Jewish characters, including one—Malvolio, in *Twelfth Night*—who is ridiculed for being a Christian.

When Shylock learns that Antonio does not have the money to meet the terms of that bond, he says: "There I have another bad match, a bankrupt, a prodigal..." (3.2.41-42). Shylock wants his money, but it would be an oversimplification to characterize him only as a miser. In addition to thrift, Shylock represents everything that comedy subverts: family, law, the established social order, sober responsibility, rightful authority, the sanctity of a bond—in short, the values that ancient Roman honor equates with flesh and blood. When Jessica escapes from Shylock's house, Shylock states plainly that he considers her breach of honor to be ultimately an offense against flesh and blood. "My own flesh and blood to rebel!" (1.1.32), he fumes. Solanio responds lewdly. "Out upon it, old carrion; rebels it at these years?" (1.1.33-34), he says, deliberately misconstruing Shylock's commitment to the family bond for its antithesis—

spontaneous sexual desire. Shylock ignores this double entendre and states unequivocally what he means: "I say my daughter is my flesh and blood" (3.1.35).

Shylock's attitude is not uniquely Jewish; it is typical of the Venetian property owner. In *Othello*, Brabantio calls it "treason of the blood" when his daughter, Desdemona, flees his house to elope with Othello: "O Heaven! How gets she out? O treason of the blood!" (*Oth.*, I.ii.169).

Comic characters like Solanio see what Shylock does and hear what he says, but have no sympathy or understanding for Shylock's moral perspective:

> I never heard a passion so confused,
> So strange, outrageous, and so variable,
> As the dog Jew did utter in the streets:
> 'My daughter! O my ducats! O my daughter!
> Fled with a Christian! O my Christian ducats!
> Justice! The law! My ducats and my daughter!'   (2.8.12-17)

Solanio asserts that Shylock is "confused" and that his behavior is "so variable." But to the contrary, Shylock's behavior is far from "variable." He remains constant in his commitment to his bonds, both familial and financial. This moral stance—which isolates him from the other characters in the play—is consistent both with Shylock's comic function as the *idiotes* in this play, and with beliefs common to Venetian property owners. Iago uses words similar to Shylock's when he wants to provoke Brabantio's rage in *Othello*: "Thieves! Thieves! Look to your house, your daughter, and your bags!," (*Oth.*, I.i.79-80). Far from being confused and variable, Shylock is as predictable as Iago expects Brabantio to be when he loses his daughter to a man he would not have chosen for her. The cry "O my ducats! O my daughter!" reflects the Venetian property owner's belief that both his daughter and his ducats are the property of his household. This belief is neither uniquely personal to Shylock nor uniquely Jewish in any way, despite the perceptions of Shylock's antagonists in the play.

For Shylock, daughter and ducat represent the bonds that are at once the basis of civilized society and the foil to festive mockery. From his perspective, these bonds—property, family and law—daughter and ducats—share a common denominator in flesh and blood. Shylock's commitment to non-festive principles is evident in is readiness to die for his property. He does not want the Duke of Venice's mercy. "Nay, take my life and all! Pardon not that! / You take my house when you do take the prop / That doth sustain my house" (4.1.370-372). To Shylock, Antonio's default on the terms of his loan has a common denominator to Jessica's escape from Shylock's household: both violate a legal bond based on property rights, which (in turn) represent moral value. Daughter and ducats, in this respect, are similar to Antonio and ducats. Having lost his own "flesh and blood" through Jessica's escape from his house, Shylock resolves that he will in turn cause bleeding by enforcing his bond with Antonio.

Shylock's desire for bloody justice is typical of Venetian men of property and is neither uniquely Jewish nor unique to Shylock's personality characteristics. In *Othello*, the Duke of Venice threatens to enforce the "letter" of the "bloody book of law" when he hears Brabantio's complaint that Desdemona has eloped with Othello: "Whoe'er he be that in this foul proceeding / Hath thus beguil'd your daughter of herself / And you of her, the bloody book of law / You shall yourself read in the bitter letter / After your own sense...." (*Oth.*, I.iii.65-69). Brabantio the Christian is no different from Shylock the Jew in his recourse to the "letter" of Venice's "bloody book of law" in defense of his property rights. It is Venetian justice that is "bloody" for both of them, not Jewish morality or Shylock's personal cruelty. However, Venetian law is neither just nor cruel in itself; its value is determined by the contextual paradigm within which it is perceived. While both Shylock and

Brabantio would shed blood to enforce a bond based upon flesh and blood, Shylock is vilified and Brabantio is not. The difference between their two situations is not Shylock's Jewishness *per se*, but his dramatic function within a Roman-style comedy. In comedy, law and property rights are vilified and ridiculed, while these values are respected in tragedy.

What the mask reveals:
Rosalind *vis à vis* Portia

The typical structure of Shakespearean comedy has three phases, according to Northrop Frye.[89] The first phase "begins with an anticomic society, a social organization blocking and opposed to the comic drive, which the action of comedy evades or overcomes."[90] This "anticomic theme" is introduced by comic characters in a melancholy mood; Frye identifies such characters in *All's Well That Ends Well, Twelfth Night, A Comedy of Errors,* and *Cymbeline,* as well as in *The Merchant of Venice*:

> The opening line of *The Merchant of Venice* is Antonio's: "In sooth, I know not why I am so sad," and the opening line spoken by the heroine, "By my troth, Nerissa, my little body is aweary of this great world," is in counterpoint with it....[91]

Frye's second phase of Shakespearean comedy is a "period of confusion and sexual license that we may call the phase of temporarily lost identity."[92] Frye notes that:

> In a sense ... all braggarts or hypocrites ... are disguised until exposed. But consistently with the main theme of comedy, the loss of identity is most frequently a loss of sexual identity. The motif of a heroine disguising herself as a boy appears in five of the comedies, there being three such disguises in *The Merchant of Venice* [Portia, Nerissa and Jessica].[93]

The confusions and disguises of the second phase are resolved in Frye's third phase, which he calls "the phase of the discovery of identity."[94] The resolution phase clarifies who has been hidden behind which mask. But it also often includes an element of self-discovery, in which "an individual comes to know himself in a way that he did not before."[95]

In several important respects, *The Merchant of Venice* follows the pattern identified by Frye. Bassanio's need for money is typical of Frye's first phase. His heavy debts are an anti-comic intrusion of reality that represents a potential threat to his festive happiness; Antonio's bond with Shylock similarly represents the unwelcome reality of anti-comic society, which poses its challenge to hoped-for festive happiness. It is in Frye's third phase, the phase of discovery, when Bassanio and Graziano learn something new: that fidelity to a promise is much more important than they had previously thought. But paradoxically it is in the so-called phase of confusion, Frye's second phase, where the play's moral issues are clarified.

The phase of confusion is decisive for the meaning of *The Merchant of Venice* because of the way in which it illuminates the truth about Bassanio's character. Fidelity to a promise—keeping one's word—is a key touchstone of character. This issue stands out in sharper relief when the second phase of *The Merchant of Venice* is compared to the second phase of *As You Like It*.[96] In both of these plays, a comic character is involved in a situation of identity confusion, typical of Frye's second stage of "temporarily lost identity." Rosalind, in *As You Like It*, assumes the disguise of a young man called Ganymede. In this disguise—which Orlando never sees through (love is blind)—"Ganymede" is frank about his intent to "cure" Orlando of his love (III.ii.424-425) for Rosalind. Ganymede challenges Orlando, questioning and testing his loyalty to Rosalind, but Orlando never deviates from his devotion to her. Through this process, Rosalind comes to see the integrity in Orlando's love for her because—in her disguise as a boy—she sees that what Orlando says about her behind her back is the same love that he professes to her face. While in disguise, Rosalind is able to prove to her satisfaction that Orlando is a solid and reliable marriage prospect.

Like Rosalind, Portia in *The Merchant of Venice* disguises herself as a young man. However, unlike Rosalind, Portia is already married to the man she loves—and what she hears her husband say about her behind her back could not be more different from what Rosalind had heard under similar circumstances: "Antonio, I am married to a wife / Which is as dear to me as life itself," Bassanio says:

> But life itself, my wife, and all the world
> Are not with me esteemed above thy life.
> I would lose all, ay, sacrifice them all
> Here to this devil, to deliver you.   (4.1.279-284)

The message is clear: Portia is expendable, although evidently Antonio is not. "Your wife would give you little thanks for that, / If she were by to hear you make the offer," Portia replies (4.1.285-286).

(Some critics have presumed there is an element of homosexuality in Bassanio's relationship with Antonio.[97] It is clear that Bassanio puts Portia second to Antonio, but while an implied homosexual relationship between the two might explain some of Bassanio's behavior, it is an unnecessary complication to Bassanio and Antonio's relationship as blood relatives. Bassanio is first mentioned in the play as Antonio's "most noble kinsman" (1.1.57), a reference that defines their close, affectionate relationship as family, not as lovers, as some have suggested.)

Graziano, whose situation echoes Bassanio's, is also quick to say he'd rather see his wife dead, if her death could save Antonio. (No one supposes that Graziano also has a homosexual relationship with Antonio because, like Bassanio, he values Antonio's life above his wife's.) "I have a wife who, I protest, I love. / I would she were in heaven, so she could/

Entreat some power to change this currish Jew" (4.1.287-289). Nerissa replies: "'Tis well you offer it behind her back; / The wish would make else an unquiet house" (4.1.290-291).

In fact, wishing that one's wife were dead is a standard joke that is typical of Plautus.[98] In Roman comedy, husbands frequently prayed that their wives would die quickly, "often adding religious blasphemy to filial or conjugal impiety.... Such mockery of religious practice impugns still another important aspect of pietas, devotion to the gods," according to Segal.[99] But however common this practice may be in Roman comedy, it is a gesture that is difficult to explain if one is predisposed to project the positive attributes of sincere, romantic affection onto Bassanio and Gratiano, who could just as easily have expressed their concern for Antonio's life without expressing a preference for their wives' deaths. Each of them has disavowed his personal commitment to his wife in a completely gratuitous way. In contrast, Orlando had refused to disavow his love for Rosalind, even though the disguised-Rosalind many times prods him to do so. Frye's "phase two" comic irony reveals Orlando to be a man of integrity, but exposes Bassanio and Graziano as deceitful and unfaithful.[100]

Other points of comparison between *The Merchant of Venice* and *As You Like It* are also instructive. One similarity is that both Rosalind and Portia identify their men with Hercules, the ancient Roman hero. Prior to the wrestling match in act one, Rosalind encourages Orlando by saying: "Now Hercules be thy speed young man!" (*AYL*, I.ii.222). In like manner, Portia encourages Bassanio in act three, prior to his choosing among the caskets: "Now he goes, / With no less presence... / Than young Alcides [Hercules].... / Go Hercules!" (*MV*, 3.2.53-60). However, although both Orlando and Bassanio are perceived as ancient Roman heroes by their women, there are several significant differences between them.

First, both Orlando and Bassanio are poor, but they are poor for very different reasons. Bassanio has piled debt upon debt by living a more lavish lifestyle than he could afford, while Orlando has had poverty forced upon him by his elder brother, Oliver. "What prodigal portion have I spent that I should come to such penury," Orlando complains to his brother (*AYL*, I.i.41-42).[101]

Second, Orlando is more sensitive to the nuances of romance. He woos Rosalind with poetry, professions of love and promises of devotion. He goes through the forest posting his poems to her on trees, for all to see. In contrast, Bassanio doesn't pine for Portia, and he writes no poetry. He is much more pragmatic. He has positive things to say about Portia, but speaks of her beauty and her money simultaneously: "In Belmont is a lady richly left,/ And she is fair ..." (1.1.161-162). Orlando speaks a great deal more of his beloved than Bassanio does. He may be as poor as Bassanio, but he never mentions Rosalind's wealth as an opportunity for personal enrichment.

Third, the characters in *The Merchant of Venice* are far less magnanimous to their adversary, Shylock, than Orlando is to his adversary, Oliver. Orlando had had good reason to hate his brother, Oliver, who had left him impoverished. However, Orlando nevertheless puts aside his resentment, saving Oliver's life while risking his own in a battle with a lioness. "Twice he did turn his back...," Oliver tells Rosalind, "But kindness, nobler ever than revenge, / And nature, stronger than his just occasion, / Made him give battle to the lioness" (IV.iii.128-131).

In contrast, the Christians show little empathy for the defeated Shylock. "Beg that thou mayst have leave to hang thyself," Graziano says to Shylock:

> And yet, thy wealth being forfeit to the state,
> Thou hast not left the value of a cord;
> Therefore thou must be hanged at the state's charge.
> (4.1.360-364)

None of the Christians rebuke Graziano for speaking with this venomous hatred. They think nothing of it. When Portia asks Antonio, "What mercy can you render him [Shylock]," Graziano responds hotly, perhaps holding a hangman's noose: "A halter, gratis. Nothing else, for God's sake!" (4.1.374-375). (Situations such as this one make it difficult to justify interpretations that idealize the Christians by contrasting Jewish revenge with Christian mercy.) Antonio's response to Portia sounds mild in comparison to Graziano's vituperation: he suggests forced conversion to Christianity and confiscation of Shylock's wealth (including a hefty inheritance for Lorenzo, who has already raided Shylock's treasury.) This response is perfect as a comic reversal, but it is not an example of mercy.

The most important difference between Orlando and Bassanio is that Bassanio fails a test of fidelity that Orlando passes. Bassanio slanders his love for his wife by wishing that she were dead, and then breaks his promise never to remove the ring that signified his bond to her. Orlando steadfastly maintains his fidelity to his word and to his wife. It is worth repeating in this context that *The Merchant of Venice*, unlike *As You Like It*, "deals with the breaking of the marriage bond, not a bond between lovers, [which] is a crucial difference."[102]

Orlando—in sharp contrast to Bassanio—demonstrates the ultimate degree of integrity according to the standard of ancient Roman honor as defined by Brutus' Portia: he sends evidence of his own torn flesh as proof of his total commitment to his word. Orlando's brother arrives with a "bloody napkin" (IV.iii.138)—a bandage soaked in his blood.[103] After fighting the lioness to save his brother's life, Orlando faints from loss of blood, but sends Oliver in his place, to tell his story:

> Here upon his arm
> The lioness had torn some flesh away,
> Which all this while had bled; and now he fainted,
> And cried, in fainting, upon Rosalind.....
> He sent me hither, stranger as I am,
> To tell this story, that you might excuse

His broken promise, and to give this napkin,
Dyed in his blood, unto the shepherd youth
That he in sport doth call his Rosalind.   (IV.iii.147-157)

Orlando's "broken promise" was the promise to arrive at his appointment with Rosalind at exactly 2 p.m. However, the tearing of flesh and blood, as in *Julius Caesar*, is proof of the highest degree of honor, a gesture well above and beyond merely showing up on time, at the exact minute promised. In effect, Orlando sends his own blood as a proxy for himself, as a metaphor for the nobility that he embodies. Orlando passes his test of fidelity *summa cum laude*: love, mercy and honor together have triumphed over the spirit of revenge. He attains this moral stature only after rising above the resentment that he felt toward his brother at the beginning of the play, elevating the imperative to duty—duty even to the point of self-sacrifice—above his own self-interest. Bassanio, in contrast, never goes beyond the limits of his self-interest. But Orlando specifically identifies "honor above self-interest" as an aspect of ancient Roman honor. "O good old man," he says at the beginning of the play:

...how well in thee appears
The constant service of the antique world,
When service sweat for duty, not meed!
Thou are not for the fashion of these times,
Where none will sweat but for promotion.   (II.iii.56-60)

The letter of the law

While disguised as legal scholars, Portia and Nerissa witness Bassanio and Graziano declare that they would like to see their wives dead. Shortly afterward, they see Bassanio and Graziano give away their wedding rings, which both men had solemnly promised never to remove. The two women confront their husbands on this breach of fidelity in the play's fifth act.

They are holding in their possession the wedding rings that their husbands gave away—the "smoking gun" evidence that proves to Bassanio and Graziano that their wives have seen them as they are. At the end of act five, Bassanio and Graziano are finally forced to admit their guilt and they beg their wives for forgiveness. Nevertheless, despite their apologies for their confessed misdeeds, some critics still seek to make excuses for Bassanio and Graziano—to idealize these characters in terms of Christian generosity, as if broken promises and infidelity were merely another variant of Christian virtue:

> When Bassanio rewards the young Doctor of Laws with Portia's ring, he is keeping the spirit of his vow to her as certainly as he would have been breaking it if he had kept the ring on his finger. In the circumstances, literal fidelity would have been actual faithlessness.[104]

According to this rationale, fidelity and faithlessness are interchangeable, depending upon the perspective of the person who defines those terms, as in *Alice in Wonderland*. However, even from this relativist moral perspective, it's difficult to understand how Bassanio could have been "*keeping* the spirit of his vow" [emphasis added] when he gave away the ring because he had already violated the spirit of that promise when he said he'd gladly sacrifice Portia's life to save Antonio. Putting friendship above marriage is a moral choice that cannot be justified without contradicting the premise that marriage vows are of primary importance. Bassanio's situation is such that he cannot be said to have been completely loyal to both his friend and his wife; his faithfulness to his friend contradicts his fidelity to his wife.

From the perspective of the Jewish/Christian interpretive paradigm, keeping to the terms of a bond or a promise is sometimes denigrated as rigid literalism, which—along with hatred, revenge and greed—is an attribute associated with Shylock, Jews and Old Testament religion. In contrast, Christianity and the New Testament allegedly consider the "spirit" of the law to be a more exalted virtue than the literalism of its "letter." However, in *As You Like It* where this issue has no Jewish or Old Testament connotation, Shakespeare is quite definite that rigid literalism is a virtue, while anything less than exact compliance or total fidelity is a sorry excuse for lack of honor. When Orlando is slightly late for his planned meeting with Rosalind (in her disguise as Ganymede), she upbraids him for lack of sincerity (*AYL*, IV.i.36-38). "My fair Rosalind," Orlando replies, "I come within an hour of my promise" (*AYL*, IV.i.42-43). But Rosalind will by no means accept anything less than total and complete commitment to the exact "letter" of his word:

> Break an hour's promise in love? He that will divide a minute into a thousand parts and break but a part of the thousandth part of a minute in the affairs of love, it may be said of him that Cupid hath clapped him o' th' shoulder, but I'll warrant him heart-whole.
> **Orlando**: Pardon me, dear Rosalind.
> **Rosalind**: Nay, an you be so tardy, come no more in my sight. (*AYL*, IV.i.44-52)

At the conclusion of their meeting, Rosalind once again emphasizes that promises of love are credible only to the extent that they are kept literally, precisely and exactly. He promises to meet her at 2 p.m., to which she replies:

> By my troth, and in good earnest, and so God mend me, and by all pretty oaths that are not dangerous, if you break one jot of your promise or come one minute behind your hour, I will think you the most pathetical break-promise, and the most hollow lover, and the most unworthy or her you call Rosalind, that may be chosen out of the gross band of the unfaithful. Therefore beware my censure and keep your promise.
> **Orlando**: With no less religion than if thou wert indeed my Rosalind. (IV.i.179-189)

Orlando does not recognize Rosalind behind her disguise as Ganymede, but he nevertheless commits himself to an extreme degree of faithfulness, "with no less religion" than if the young lad Ganymede were in fact Rosalind. Rosalind postulates a literalist, absolutist, all-or-nothing standard that says you are either completely true to your word or you are completely false. She demands an inflexible, exact fidelity to the most trivial of promises, according to which she gauges faithfulness to the most non-trivial of commitments. Unless Orlando can arrive at his appointment with absolutely precise punctuality, his personal integrity is immediately called into question.

Lorenzo in *The Merchant of Venice* is completely untrustworthy, according to Rosalind's standard of exact punctuality as gauge of faithfulness. He does not arrive at the appointed time for his elopement with Shylock's daughter, Jessica, whom he is supposed to help escape from her father's house. Presumably Lorenzo is madly in love with Jessica and can hardly wait for the moment when she will run away with him. But he is late—by nearly an hour. His friends, who arrive on time, are waiting for him under Jessica's window, wondering how he could be late for this important rendezvous with the woman he is supposed to be deeply in love with:

> **Graziano:** This is the penthouse under which Lorenzo
> Desired us to make stand.
> **Salarino:** His hour is almost past.
> **Graziano:** And it is marvel he out-dwells his hour,
> For lovers ever run before the clock.
> **Salarino:** O ten times faster Venus' pigeons fly
> To seal love's bonds new made than they are wont
> To keep obliged faith unforfeited.
> **Graziano:** That ever holds. Who riseth from a feast
> With that keen appetite that he sits down? (2.6.1-9)

If he is as much in love with her as he is presumed to be, his lateness for his own elopement just doesn't make sense. As Salarino and Graziano's conversation continues, Jessica presumably waits silently by the window, sitting patiently for nearly an hour beside Shylock's money chest, which she plans to toss down to Lorenzo if and when he finally shows up.

Lorenzo doesn't give much explanation for his tardiness. He simply says "Sweet friends, your patience for my long abode" (2.6.21). He does not take responsibility for his lateness, offering the vague excuse that "Not I but my affairs have made you wait" (2.6.22). He says that he would wait for them under similar circumstances, implying that there is nothing unusual about being nearly an hour late for one's own elopement: "When you shall please to play the thieves for wives / I'll watch as long for you then" (2.6.23-24).

There is something fundamentally wrong with interpretations of *The Merchant of Venice* that persist in believing that the Christian characters in the play represent true love and loyalty, despite ample evidence of their insensitivity, unreliability and bad faith. The undeniable fact of Lorenzo's lateness is an anomaly that has no meaning in the context of the Christian/Jewish interpretive paradigm. It does not enhance the presumed generosity of spirit, love and friendship that are supposedly characteristic of the play's Christians. Even Lorenzo's friends find his lateness for his own elopement inexplicable. However, Lorenzo's lateness makes perfect sense in the context of the honor/irony interpretive paradigm, which emphasizes the importance of keeping one's word exactly and precisely. His tardiness illustrates that he does not keep his promises; it shows him to be an ignoble character in the Plautine pattern. His tardiness directly contradicts the demanding standard of trustworthiness postulated by Rosalind in *As You Like It*—a standard similar in severity to that of ancient Roman honor, as articulated by Brutus in *Julius Caesar*:

> ...every drop of blood
> That every Roman bears, and nobly bears,
> Is guilty of a several bastardy,
> *If he do break the smallest particle*
> *Of any promise that hat pass'd from him.*   (*JC*, II.136-140)
> [Italics added for emphasis]

Desdemona, in *Othello*, is similarly rigid in her commitment to a promise: to speak up for Cassio, even though Othello may not want to hear her praise Cassio.[105] Clearly rigid fidelity to a promise is a moral virtue in Shakespeare plays where this issue is not associated with Jews or Old Testament religion.

The words used by the disguised Rosalind in the first scene of act four in *As You Like It* mirror those of the disguised Portia in the first scene of act four in *The Merchant of Venice*. Rosalind admonishes Orlando not to break "one jot" (IV.i.194) of his promise, while Portia had insisted that Shylock's bond entitled him to "no jot" of blood (*MV*, 4.1.303). Where Rosalind insists upon fidelity to "a part of the thousandth part of a minute," Portia demands fidelity to "the division of the twentieth part/ Of one poor scruple" (*MV*, 4.1.325-326). Despite their use of similar words, however, they use these words toward ends that are antithetical: Rosalind invokes literal exactitude to hold Orlando accountable to the highest possible standard of personal commitment; Portia, on the other hand, invokes literal exactitude to help get Antonio off the hook and escape from the terms of a solemn legal bond.

While Portia might have been expected to speak of a "drop" of blood, instead she speaks of a "jot" of blood, which more strongly suggests literal fidelity to the letter of a promise. "Jot," a tiny particle, derives from "iota," the ninth letter in the Greek alphabet; the word is used in the New Testament.[106] The King James Version says:

> Think not that I am come to destroy the law, or the prophets: I am not come to destroy, but to fulfill. For verily I say unto you, Till heaven and earth pass, one jot [*The Geneva Bible* uses the word 'iote' instead of 'jot'] or one tittle shall in no wise pass from the law, till all be fulfilled. (*Matt. 5:17-18*)

In this passage from the Sermon on the Mount, Jesus stipulates that the law should be observed exactly and precisely, until the Kingdom of Heaven comes to pass on Earth. Rosalind's insistence on literal fidelity to a promise in love—"If you break one jot of your promise ...I will think you the most pathetical break-promise" (*AYL*, IV.i.194-195)—is therefore similar in spirit to Jesus' demand that the Jews be zealous in keeping to the exact letter of God's covenant with them. Jesus, in his own words, emphasizes the importance of literal fidelity to the written law. In the context in which He uses the word "jot," Jesus is not abolishing the law with a new covenant of mercy. Neither is He suggesting that the "spirit" of the law should supersede its "letter." Instead, He is taking the law one step further: "Whosoever therefore shall break the least of these commandments, and shall teach men so, he shall be called the least in the kingdom of heaven" (Matt. 5:19). Rosalind, like Jesus, insists that even the *least* violation of a promise is totally unacceptable.

To be called "least in the kingdom of heaven" for breaking the "least" of the commandments is even more stringent—less forgiving and less merciful—than the Jewish morality that had preceded the Sermon on the Mount. That Jesus was a proponent of a literal legalism who would not change the letter of the law "one jot" and who would severely condemn the violation of even "the least of these commandments" undermines the supposed dichotomy of harsh, Jewish legalism and gentle Christian mercy that has been a basic premise of traditional *Merchant of Venice* criticism within the Christian/Jewish interpretive paradigm.

While it is no doubt a cruel law that would punish a debtor for defaulting on a loan, it is an even harsher morality that would pluck out an eye or cut off a hand because of an immoral *thought*:

> If thy right eye offend thee, pluck it out, and cast it from thee: for it is profitable for thee that one of thy members should perish, and not that thy whole body should be cast into hell. And if thy right hand offend thee, cut it off, and cast it from thee: for it is profitable for thee that one of they members should perish, and not that thy whole body should be cast into hell. *(Matt. 5:29-30)*

This self-punishing self-restraint resembles ancient Roman honor as it was personified by Portia, who mutilated her own thigh—not in punishment for violating a trust, but premeptively, as proof that no violation of trust would take place. The severely-demanding Christian morality of the Sermon on the Mount, then, seems to be similar in spirit to the sharp demands of ancient Roman honor as stipulated by Rosalind in *As You Like It* and as personified by Portia in *Julius Caesar*. Jewish morality, more lenient by comparison, is irrelevant to Shakespeare's map of comparative of morality, which is defined by two poles—Christian morality and ancient Roman honor, both of which stipulate exact fidelity to the letter of a bond.

This moral perspective is defined between two sharply antithetical extremes: either total order or total chaos; either unswerving fidelity or complete disloyalty; there is no middle-of-the-road morality of moderation between the two extremes. Honor is the absolutist, all-or-nothing moral commitment that is the only alternative to the anything-goes, everything-is-excusable, relativist, liberality of festive license. The strain of Christian morality that reflects this perspective is the eschatological, apocalyptic morality preached by Jesus himself in the Synoptic Gospels—Mark, Matthew and Luke. This morality originated at a point in time that marked the convergence of two extremes—the end point of prophetic Judaism and the beginning point of Christianity. Paradoxically, it is Christian morality at that historical moment when it was most Jewish, when Christianity was still a Jewish sect, before it had become a distinct religion in its own right.

In sum, it is a false dichotomy to suppose that the "spirit" of a promise and the "letter" of that promise could be two different things; further, it is inaccurate to cast this false dichotomy in Christian/Jewish terms. Honor and fidelity to a bond—fidelity to the letter, and therefore to the spirit—are all inter-

twined together, along with love and mercy, for Christianity
as well as for ancient Roman honor. And love, forgiveness and
literal fidelity are together guaranteed by flesh and blood, in
romance, no less than in business. Orlando measures up to
the "letter" of these standards, but Bassanio does not. And
Bassanio's failure to do so cannot be excused on religious
grounds, simply because he hates Shylock, the Jew.

Part two

The logic of inverse irony

Bassanio's meditation on the three caskets is the play's most comprehensive exposition of the proposition that superficial appearance is deceptive—that what appears to be most self-evident is actually that which is most illusory. This speech at the centerpoint of the play begins with the statement that "outward shows be least themselves. / The world is still deceived with ornament" (3.2.73-74). Bassanio does not merely concede the possibility that external appearances could be misleading; instead he states definitively and authoritatively that superficial appearance is the most extreme antithesis to the truth, and that the truth is hidden beneath the surface. "Outward shows be *least* themselves," he says [emphasis added]. He then gives several examples: vice appears to be virtue; cowards appear to be heroes; "fair ornament" hides "grossness." Outward show—superficial appearance—(in Bassanio's view) is that which is *least* true; the actual truth—which is hidden beneath the surface—is that which *least* resembles outward appearance.

The truth, according to this perspective, is the extreme antithesis to what superficially appears to be true. For the sake of convenience, we will define the logic of this perspective as inverse irony, which should be understood as the most extreme extension of Roman comedy's festive irony.

Bassanio's meditation on the three caskets methodically applies the principle of inverse irony to the issues raised throughout the play: an interpretation of law, the truth of a religious belief, the perception of a man's virtue, the perception of a woman's beauty. This speech, quoted here in full, is more important to the meaning of the play than any other single passage:

> So may the outward shows be least themselves.
> The world is still deceived with ornament.
> In law, what plea so tainted and corrupt
> But, being seasoned with a gracious voice,
> Obscures the show of evil? In religion,
> What damned error but some sober brow
> Will bless it and approve it with a text,
> Hiding the grossness with fair ornament?
> There is no vice so simple but assumes
> Some mark of virtue on his outward parts.
> How many cowards, whose hearts are all as false
> As stairs of sand, wear yet upon their chins
> The beards of Hercules and frowning Mars,
> Who inward searched have livers white as milk?
> And these assume but valour's excrement
> To render them redoubted. Look on beauty,
> And you shall see 'tis purchas'd by the weight,
> Which therein works a miracle in nature,
> Making them lightest that wear most of it.
> So are those crisped, snaky, golden locks
> Which makes such wanton gambols with the wind
> Upon supposed fairness, often known
> To be the dowry of a second head,
> The skull that bred them in the sepulchre.
> Thus ornament is but the guiled shore
> To a most dangerous sea, the beauteous scarf
> Veiling an Indian beauty; in a word,
> The seeming truth which cunning times put on
> To entrap the wisest.   (3.2.73-101)

Like Bassanio, Antonio articulates the festive logic of inverse irony. "The devil can cite Scripture to his purpose," Antonio says:

> An evil soul producing holy witness
> Is like a villain with a smiling cheek,
> A goodly apple rotten at the heart.
> O what a goodly outside falsehood hath!   (1.3.95-99)

According to Antonio, two extremes—good and evil—can easily be mistaken for one another because superficial beauty can hide an ugly reality.[107] A shiny red apple rotten at the core symbolizes the paradox of inverse irony, which is also the main lesson taught by the challenge of the three caskets: what is golden on the outside is worthless on the inside; what is ugly, worthless lead on the outside contains the beauteous Portia and her fortune on the inside.

According to the logic of inverse irony, inside and outside are extreme opposites, and outward appearance is routinely deceptive, such that the unenlightened observer will find nothing where he expects to find treasure. The enlightened observer—Bassanio, for example—knows that treasure hides behind that which appears to be worthless. The three caskets teach this lesson three times—once for each of the two unsuccessful suitors, and once following Bassanio's successful selection of the casket made of lead.

The first casket, selected by the unfortunate Prince of Morocco, teaches:

> All that glisters is not gold;
> Often have you heard that told.
> Many a man his life hath sold
> But my outside to behold.
> Gilded tombs do worms infold.   (2.7.65-69)

Gold on the outside; worms on the inside. A perfect example of inverse irony.

The second casket, selected by the similarly unfortunate Prince of Arragon, proves that silver can be as misleading as gold:

> Some there be that shadows kiss;
> Such have but a shadow's bliss.
> There be fools alive, iwis,
> Silvered o'er, and so was this.   (2.9.65-68)

The third casket, made of lead—and correctly chosen by Bassanio—contains a message similar to those in the other caskets:

> You that choose not by the view,
> Chance as fair and choose as true!
> Since this fortune falls to you,
> Be content, and seek no new.   (3.2.131-134)

All three caskets say: don't believe external appearance. Furthermore, the song that is sung while Bassanio considers which casket to choose also reiterates this message.

> Tell me where is fancy bred,
> Or in the heart, or in the head?...
> It is engendered in the eyes,
> With gazing fed...   (3.2.63-71)

Here, in the centerpiece of the play, the proposition that outward appearance is false is emphasized as forcefully as one could wish—by the song, the message of the three caskets and (most exhaustively) by Bassanio in his speech, "Outward shows be least themselves" (3.2.73). The line of reasoning explored in that speech enables Bassanio to successfully identify the correct casket among misleading alternatives and to win Portia and her fortune: Bassanio needs gold, but knows enough to mistrust appearance. He considers that "outward shows be least themselves" and therefore selects the casket that looks least like gold, thereby becoming a wealthy man.

It is trivial to suggest, as some commentators have done, that the song, "Where is fancy bred," is Portia's way a giving Bassanio a clue as to which casket to select. Bassanio's lengthy speech on outward show makes it quite clear that he doesn't need any clues: he thoroughly understands the lesson of the caskets. He makes the correct choice because he knows with surgical precision that the truth is most often *least* like that which outwardly appears to be true. More significant than whether the song gives Bassanio a clue to the correct casket is: what clue does Bassanio give readers about the meaning of the play? He has picked the correct casket because he knows how to deduce truth from misleading appearances. How does he do it? What rationale does he use to determine what is true in a world in which appearance is illusory? Granting the assumption that human perception is unreliable and that appearances are false, what can Bassanio tell the reader about how to recognize what is true, despite a deceptive facade? Bassanio's fundamental premise is the principle of inverse irony, which finds the truth to be antithetical to that which superficially appears to be obviously true. Inverse irony is a festive logic that believes superficial appearance to be the extreme opposite to what is actually true.

According to the logic of inverse irony that Bassanio expounds, "in law" a "gracious voice" can season to advantage a plea that is "tainted and corrupt." Applying this logic to the interpretation of *The Merchant of Venice*, there is reason to be suspicious of any legal ruling that is justified with impressive-sounding legalisms. Portia appropriates a seemingly-plausible, scholarly-sounding legal rationale to save Antonio from Shylock's knife. But her gracious voice is the festive mask that hides a corruption of Roman law.

The logic of inverse irony inverts the meaning of Portia's statement: "O, these naughty times/ Put bars between the owners and their rights" (3.2.18-19). Portia's remark about "these naughty times" ostensibly expresses her sense of impatience that Bassanio must first pass the test of the caskets before he can marry her. However, according to the logic of festive irony, her comment indicates that the "naughty times" (that is to say, festive holiday inversions) violate conventional property rights—not Portia's own property rights, to be sure, but those of Shylock, her moral and social antithesis, who under non-festive circumstances would have had a valid legal claim to both Antonio's flesh and his own property.

As Antonio's "most noble kinsman" (1.1.57), Bassanio is a

blood relation to Antonio, who in turn is a literary relative to a
family that traced its patronym back to a son of Hercules called
Anton. Portia invokes this heritage just as Bassanio is about to
ponder his choice between the caskets:

> Now he goes,
> With no less presence but with much more love
> Than young Alcides [i.e., Hercules], when he did redeem
> The virgin tribute paid by howling Troy
> To the sea-monster....
> ... Go, Hercules.   (3.2.53-60)

But according to the festive logic of inverse irony that Bassanio
articulates, the one who looks most like a hero (such as Hercules) may in fact be the one who is least heroic: "How many
cowards, whose hearts are all as false / As stairs of sand, wear
yet upon their chins / The beards of Hercules and frowning
Mars...?" (3.2.83-85). Following so shortly after Portia's characterization of him as a Hercules, Bassanio's statement clearly
implies that he himself may be the one who is least noble because he, more than anyone, outwardly resembles Hercules.

By the same token, Portia's beauty—her long blond hair—
may be a surface distraction that masks her true nature. "Those
crisped, snaky, golden locks....[are] often known / To be the
dowry of a second head, / The skull that bred them in the sepulchre," Bassanio says (3.2.92-96). Bassanio's speculation that
beauty might be a false front adds resonance to the irony later,
when he opens the lead casket and exclaims: "Fair Portia's
counterfeit!" (3.2.115).

When Antonio says "the devil can cite Scripture for his purpose" (1.3.95), he is speaking of Shylock, who is telling his
story about Jacob and Laban (1.3.68-87). However, according
to Antonio's own opinion about the inverse relationship between appearance and reality, this statement is more appli-
cable to Shylock's antagonists—who cite Scripture for their own
festive, fundamentally irreligious purposes—than to Shylock

himself.

Most importantly, when Bassanio states that "in religion," the "grossness" of a "damned error" could be hidden by "fair ornament," it is a warning not to be misled by a religious sentiment that is presented in flowery, poetic language. Portia's famous speech on the quality of mercy affects a spiritual-sounding tone, but it is the "fair ornament" that justifies pagan hedonism, which is "damned error"—or from the perspective of Christian religion, a damnable error.

In general, the "goodly outside" in *The Merchant of Venice* is the lofty-sounding talk about love and mercy typical of the Christian characters. Whatever Shylock's flaws may be, presenting a "goodly outside" isn't one of them. Antonio's comment that "the devil can cite Scripture for his purpose" echoes Bassanio's statement that a "sober brow" can bless and approve with text a "damned error" in religion, hiding "grossness with fair ornament" (3.2.77-79). Together, these comments signal that Portia's fine speech on the quality of mercy just might be a pious fraud, a festive deceit.

Antonio/Shylock

Considering Bassanio's extended poetic articulation of the premise that outward appearance is "*least*" itself, it is significant that only 200 lines later he says that Antonio is the "one in whom / The ancient Roman honour *more appears* / Than any that draws breath in Italy" [emphasis added] (3.2.292-294). Although Bassanio could have said that Antonio *is* the foremost personification of ancient Roman honor, he doesn't phrase his statement quite so definitively. Instead he says that "the ancient Roman honor *more appears*" in Antonio than in anyone else. According to the principle of inverse irony—the rationale that Bassanio successfully applied (in the test of the three caskets) to discover the truth that hides beneath superficial appearance—it would be logical to conclude that Antonio's moral character might actually be antithetical to that which it most "appears" to be.

In fact, Bassanio's description of Antonio is inaccurate. The ideal of ancient Roman honor appears only faintly in Antonio, if at all. In the opening lines of the play, Antonio confesses that he is sad and weary—qualities that are distinctly contrary to the personal dynamism associated with the ideal of ancient Roman honor. Antonio begins the play with this statement:

> In sooth, I know not why I am so sad.
> It wearies me, you say it wearies you;
> But how I caught it, found it, or came by it,
> What stuff 'tis made of, whereof it is born,
> I am to learn;
> And such a want-wit sadness makes of me
> That I have much ado to know myself.   (1.1.1-7)

Ancient Romans could be weary like Antonio, but that state of mind was recognized as something short of the ancient Roman ideal. In *Julius Caesar*, Cassius says to Casca: "You are dull, Casca, and those sparks of life / That should be in a Roman you do want" (*JC*, I.iii.57-58). Cassius implies that energetic vitality is a distinctly Roman virtue, and assumes that his fellow Romans, by common consensus, would not question this belief.

Antonio's ancient Roman namesake, Marc Antony, is himself a good example of the playful vitality that is quintessentially Roman. "I am not gamesome," Brutus says to Cassius. "I do lack some of part/ of that quick spirit that is in Antony" (*JC*, I.ii.28-29). Whatever else Antonio's self-confessed state of depression might mean, it contradicts Bassanio's characterization of him as "The best-conditioned and *unwearied* spirit...in whom / The ancient Roman honour more appears / Than any that draws breath in Italy" [emphasis added] (3.2.291-293).

The discrepancy between Bassanio's characterization of Antonio and Antonio's lassitude conforms to a pattern of irony that has already been discussed in depth. Bassanio's words do not correspond with reality; more to the point, what he says is antithetical to the truth. However, if one grants the logic of Bassanio's premise that appearance is least itself, then the inverse of his statement about Antonio as an exemplar of ancient Roman honor is likely to be true, that is: the one in whom the ancient Roman honor least appears might be the one who in fact most personifies ancient Roman honor. That character would be Antonio's antagonist, Shylock, whose persona as a lowly Jewish moneylender is undoubtedly antithetical to anyone's image of an exemplar of ancient Roman honor.

Despite Shylock's identity as a Jew, in the context of his role in a Roman-style comedy, his dramatic function is undoubtedly equivalent to that of a noble Roman: he is the *paterfamilias,* the authority figure, the defender of family and property, prudent money management and sober responsibility—the enemy and foil of comic characters who drink too much liquor, squander too much money and recklessly pursue romantic fancy. Like the *patresfamilias* in Roman comedy, Shylock must yield to the festive dominance of those who travesty law, authority and the social order.

The escape of Shylock's Christian servant, Lancelot Gobbo, makes sense in this dramatic context, but would otherwise be an inexplicable anomaly: Jews living in the ghettos of Europe were not commonly permitted to employ Christians as servants. It is also an anomaly that Shylock "apparently lives in Venice proper, not in the ghetto, which is never referred to by name" in the play, as Professor Jay Halio notes.[108] Likewise, Shylock's use of the word "publican" as an epithet for Antonio—a Roman/New Testament word—is an anomaly coming from a Jew. However, most significantly, when Shylock makes his stand for law, he stands for Roman law (which punished debtors in default by cutting their flesh), not on any moral principle derived from Jewish law or tradition.

Displacing a Roman aristocrat with a Jew is an inversion that takes the logic of Roman comedy one step beyond itself, building upon Roman comedy's traditional festive role inversions by substituting an opposite inversion—a double inversion, in effect. It is a festive role reversal of the customary festive role reversal. In *The Merchant of Venice*, as in Roman comedy, the slaves invert the dominance of their masters, the *paterfamilias*, in a comic inversion of normative standards. But unlike Roman comedy, in *The Merchant of Venice*, the inverted *paterfamilias* is inverted yet again behind the persona of another extreme opposite, a Jewish money lender: where Roman comedy mocks a *paterfamilias* who represents society's power structure, *The Merchant of Venice* mocks a father figure who is a social outcast. In Shakespearean comedy, the father/authority figure is not usually the one whose identity is disguised. Yet in *The Merchant of Venice* the authority figure is the one who is most thoroughly disguised—a noble Roman hidden behind the mask of a Jewish clown.

The substitution of a Jewish money lender for a Roman aristocrat is a role reversal that is analogous to the festive reversal of roles that took place on the Saturnalia, when slaves and masters exchanged places. In both cases, opposite extremes—vanquished Jew and the conquering Roman, similar to the relationship between slaves and masters—exchange places in a festive inversion of normative reality. In addition to the historical antagonism between Romans and Jews, Jewish morality (no less than Christian morality) was antithetical to the ethos of ancient Roman honor in many respects. But these antithetical moralities nevertheless share superficial similarities that make it possible to hide Roman honor behind a Jewish mask: namely, the importance of the patriarchal family, a great respect for the law and a reputation for sobriety and prudent money management—Puritanism, generally speaking.

Shylock and Antonio are complementary antitheses, opposite sides to a single coin—inverse reflections of a common ideal that can be inferred from the play, but which the play does not reveal directly. Leslie Fiedler sees an "unsuspected kinship" between Shylock and Antonio, one "a hated Jew, the other a beloved ancient Roman," but both "almost equally alien to the world of the play."[109] And in fact Shylock, with his hooked nose, even looks something like Julius Caesar, whom Sir John Falstaff describes as "the hook-nos'd fellow of Rome" (*Henry IV, Part 2*, IV. iii. 44-45). Therefore Portia is not entirely facetious when she says upon seeing them for the first time: "Which is the merchant here, and which the Jew?" (4.1.171).[110]

Rather than merely inverting Roman values, as Roman comedy does, *The Merchant of Venice* inverts the opposite of those values, extending the rules of Roman comedy to a self-contradictory point of absurdity. Shakespeare brings the logic of festive irony full circle, to the point where a double negative—the inversion of inverse-opposites—appears equivalent to a positive. Antithetical opposites are stretched to such extremes that they converge on a single point of apparently common appearance/identity. Bright moonlight is mistaken for pale daylight, so to speak. It is another example of inverse irony: outward show is *least* itself, and the world is deceived by superficial appearance.

Ironic honesty

Bassanio delivers a fine speech on how superficial appearances deceive. In doing so, he gives the impression that he himself is sincere and trustworthy. However, Bassanio is not exempt from the inverse irony that he explains. He initially appears trustworthy to Portia, but as we have seen already, he later betrays his love for her. While in disguise, Portia learns that Bassanio is not what he had appeared to be.

Ancient Roman honor and Roman festive irony represent opposite extremes. Honor is simple, forthright and trustworthy; comic irony is more complex by comparison, playing upon the divergence between the appearance of honor and a dishonorable reality. The man of ancient Roman honor is exactly what he appears to be, down to his flesh and blood. He refuses to dissemble. But the hero of ancient Roman comedy, conversely, is frivolous in word and deed, deceptive and dishonest. He may well portray himself in various ways relative to a variety of situations, presenting an image that is fundamentally quite different from his true character, as his needs dictate.

Bassanio is a case in point. He professes not to care about money, but desperately needs some. He declares sententiously that he is not impressed by gold or silver. Nevertheless, the reality hidden beneath this exterior is that Bassanio desperately needs Portia's wealth to repay debts for which his best friend's life is at risk. Considering that Antonio's life hangs in the balance as Bassanio ponders which casket to select, his "conduct and his attitudinizing over 'ornament' are contemptible," according to Professor Philip Edwards. "He is indeed, as famously described by Quiller-Couch a 'fortune-hunter,' and a hypocrite to boot."[111]

Bassanio knows from personal experience how effectively appearances can manipulate perception. Despite his ostentatious disdain for superficial appearance, his substantial debts testify to a track record of having cultivated a wealthier image than his means could sustain. He frankly admits to Antonio that he has consistently followed a pattern of *"showing* a more swelling port [emphasis added] / Than...[his] faint means would grant continuance" (1.1.124-125).

Bassanio's concern for outward appearance extends even to his companion, Graziano, whom he advises to tone down crude personality traits:

Thou art too wild, too rude and bold of voice—

> Parts that become thee happily enough,
> And in such eyes as ours appear not faults;
> But where thou art not known, why, there they show
> Something too liberal. Pray thee, take pain
> To allay with some cold drops of modesty
> Thy skipping spirit, lest through thy wild behaviour
> I be misconstered in the place I go to,
> And lose my hopes. (2.2.173-181)

These are not the words of someone who knows only natural honesty and simple sincerity. Bassanio is quite concerned about the image he wishes to present; he has no problem with his friend's boisterous personality, but he asks Graziano to "keep a lid on it," so speak, so as not to spoil the impression that he, Bassanio, hopes to make. To use the parlance of his meditation on the three caskets, Bassanio intends to hide Graziano's negative personality traits behind an exterior of silver or gold.

Graziano responds to his suggestion with a knowing readiness to play along; he makes it clear that he understands Bassanio's game plan:

> If I do not put on a sober habit,
> Talk with respect, and swear but now and then,
> Wear prayer-books in my pocket, look demurely—
> Nay more, while grace is saying hood mine eyes
> Thus with my hat, and sigh, and say 'Amen',
> Use all the observance of civility,
> Like one well studied in a sad ostent
> To please his grandam—never trust me more. (2.2.182-189)

In effect, Graziano says: trust me to be deceptive. Bassanio is not at all offended by this attitude and offers no objection to Graziano's intended pretense because he is the one who had requested this pretense in the first place. Of course, there is a good deal of humorous exaggeration in Graziano's statement. But what shines through the jesting is both a cheerful willingness to lie and a fundamental contempt for men of prayer. This attitude is entirely appropriate to a festive attack on morality in the context of a Roman-style comedy. But Graziano's disrespect for piety contradicts the basic premise of a Christian/Jewish interpretative paradigm, which (at some level) presumes a dichotomy between Christian religiosity and Shylock the infidel, between spiritual love and material greed.

Yes, Bassanio passes the test of the caskets, which superficially appears to validate the sincerity of his profession of devotion to Portia. Nevertheless, despite the test of the caskets, Bassanio's sincerity is still suspect. "To you, Antonio,/ I owe the most in money and in love," he had said at the beginning of the play (1.1.130-131), a sentiment that is confirmed later when he expresses the wish that Portia were dead and in heaven in order to save Antonio. But if the test of caskets cannot validate Bassanio's sincerity, the inverse is true: Bassanio's insincerity proves the validity of the caskets: outward appearance is not to be believed.

As someone who has many times previously manipulated appearances for personal advantage, Bassanio is too sophisticated to blatantly reveal his financial self-interest by selecting the golden casket. As Professor Girard explains:

> Venice is a world in which appearances and reality do not match. Of all the pretenders to Portia's hand, Bassanio alone makes the right choice between the three caskets because he alone is a Venetian and knows how deceptive a splendid exterior can be. Unlike his foreign competitors who obviously come from countries where things still are more or less what they seem to be, less advanced countries, we might say, he instinctively feels that the priceless treasure he seeks must hide behind the most unlikely appearance.[112]

That Venetians are presumed to be more sophisticated than people from "less advanced countries"—especially when it comes to advancing their financial self-interest—is an assumption that is evident in *Othello*, where Iago stereotypes Desdemona and Othello respectively as "a super-subtle Venetian" and "an erring Barbarian"—terms that also could describe respectively Bassanio and any of the other men who had unsuccessfully sought Portia and her fortune. Iago also evidently assumes that money is a primary motivating factor in Venetian love and marriage. "Put but money in thy purse," Iago advises Roderigo, who covets Desdemona (*Oth.*, I.iii.351).

> Make all the money thou canst. If sanctimony and a frail vow betwixt an erring barbarian and a super-subtle Venetian be not too hard for my wits and all the tribe of hell, thou shalt enjoy her; therefore make money. (*Oth.*, I.iii.360-365).

Bassanio is one of these "super-subtle" Venetians who knows which side his bread is buttered on, so to speak, and is clever enough to say the words that will make him a rich man. He understands that "the secret of success is sincerity. Once you can fake that, you've got it made," as Hollywood film producer Samuel Goldwyn is reputed to have said. And so Bassanio passes the test of the three caskets by cloaking his own deceptiveness behind noble-sounding words about how deceptive appearances can be.[113]

The fundamental irony of Bassanio's speech on the falseness of superficial appearance is that he himself is least what he appears to be. Bassanio's speech is deceptive in the sense in which he delivers it: to imply that he personally cares little for money or external appearance and is without deceit. But his statement is true in an ironic sense: he admits that he is not what he appears to be when he states that outward show is least itself; his own outward appearance is actually farthest from that which he really is. That being the case, his words are doubly ironic: he is forthright and honest when he says that outward appearances can mislead—creating the appearance of honesty, which is deceptive. He manages to lie while telling the truth, turning the truth inside out as well as upside down. He melds appearance and reality together in an ambiguous unity of opposites that is simultaneously both true and false, grossly obvious and subtly deceptive.

Portia acknowledges Bassanio's financial interest in her (despite the ostensibly idealistic nature of their relationship) when she speaks of love in terms of money. "I would be trebled twenty times myself," Portia says:

> A thousand times more fair, ten thousand times more rich,
> That only to stand high in your account
> I might in virtues, beauties, livings, friends
> Exceed account. But the full sum of me
> In sum of something which, to term in gross,
> Is an unlessoned girl...   (3.2.153-59)

Nuttall notes that "wealth is twice placed at the summit of an ascending rhetorical scale involving character and beauty:

> The accountant's language, 'to term in gross', is uncomfortably close to what is actually going on. An imprudent director ... might well have Bassanio surprised by these words in the very act of appraising with his eye the value of the room's hangings.[114]

Nuttall says Shakespeare's "strangely bland coupling in this play of the language of love and the language of money is in a manner kidding on the level," which is to say: speaking frankly about an unpleasant truth in a jocular manner, as if it weren't true—even though it *is* true.[115] Portia's description of herself in monetary terms forthrightly states a hard fact, but does so in a soft manner; she states the truth in a way that hides the truth, even though she has spoken truthfully. Bassanio achieves the same effect in his speech on outward show, when he says outward appearance is least itself, describing himself truthfully, though in a manner that is basically deceptive.

This pattern of irony, which juxtaposes love and money, sincerity and deceptiveness, is deeply rooted in the play. For example, just as Bassanio is about to begin his speech on how appearances can deceive, Portia says to him: "Confess/ What treason there is mingled with your love....I fear you speak upon the rack,/ Where men enforced do speak anything" (3.2.26-27, 32-33). At one level, Portia's words are superficial banter; at another level, her words are an ironic challenge to Bassanio's integrity and an implied confirmation that Bassanio's love may

have in it an element of treason—that he might not be completely faithful or that he might have more of a financial interest in her than he makes apparent.[116]

Bassanio's reply is cryptic and somewhat defensive. He does
not admit to the "treason" in his love. But as an ironic prelude
to his later breach of trust with Portia, he criticizes her for her
apparent lack of trust in him:

> [There is no treason] but that ugly treason of mistrust,
> Which makes me fear th'enjoying of my love.
> There may as well be amity and life
> 'Tween snow and fire as treason and my love. (3.2.28-31)

He does not respond directly to Portia's playful challenge to
his integrity because he is too sophisticated to tell an outright
lie when instead he can weave a subtle web of extenuating
rhetoric.

In his speech on appearance, Bassanio professes to care little
for superficial things such as gold or silver. But when he asks
for the opportunity to choose between the caskets, he says:
"But let me to my fortune and the caskets" (3.2.39). "Fortune"
could simply mean "fate," but it could also mean "wealth," if
his ulterior financial motive is granted. Graziano also uses this
ambiguous word: "Your fortune stood upon the caskets there,"
he says to Bassanio (3.2.201). Graziano states that the promises of love he has exchanged with Nerissa hinge upon the
condition that "your [Bassanio's] fortune/ Achieved her mis-
tress" (3.2.207-208), again using the term "fortune" with forthright ambiguity; it could mean either fate or money—or both.
Shortly before, Graziano had used a similar ambiguity when
he spoke of Bassanio and Portia's imminent wedding as the
occasion "when your honours mean to solemnize / The bargain of your faith" (3.2.192-193), again suggesting the monetary aspect of Bassanio's interest in Portia and reinforcing
the similarity of supposed antitheses, the commerce of Venice
and the romance of Belmont.

While some interpretations of the play contrast greed (Shylock's) and generosity (Antonio's) as thematic antitheses, *The Merchant of Venice* closely links money and love together, as if they were identical, rather than opposite.[117] It does so through its use of metaphor and ambiguous words, such as "golden fleece" and "fortune," which have a meaning relevant to both money and love. Nuttall notes that:

> There was of course a convention of applying the language of finance to love, but the point of the convention lay in a paradox, the paradox of applying the lowest and most contemptible terms to the highest at the same time most human situation, love.[118]

When a letter from Antonio arrives shortly thereafter, Graziano makes plain the financial interest he and Bassanio have in Portia's wealth:

> What's the news from Venice?
> How doth that royal merchant, good Antonio?
> I know he will be glad of our success;
> We are the Jasons, we have won the fleece.   (3.2.236-239)

He exults as if he and Bassanio had just hit a lottery jackpot, as if Portia were a prize to be won—and a golden prize at that, despite having been won by means of a casket made of lead. In addition to Antonio's personal sympathy for Bassanio and Graziano, he will be glad of their success because, having just won the golden fleece, Bassanio will have the means to repay his debts to him.

The irony of honest dishonesty and forthright ambiguity is evident in Bassanio's first words upon selecting the correct casket: "Fair Portia's counterfeit!" (3.2.115), he says, referring to Portia's picture, which he finds in the casket. But the word "counterfeit" also categorizes Portia in monetary terms (similar to previous references such as " fleece" or "fortune") and suggests as well that her external appearance may be deceptive.

"Counterfeit" is (of course) fake money, deceptively passed for legal tender. Portia may be "fair," that is to say, beautiful in her physical appearance; however, Bassanio has specifically said that superficial beauty could hide less attractive qualities (3.2.92-96). She may appear to be fair in the sense of being impartial as a judge; but in this respect, outward appearance (to speak in Bassanio's terms) is least itself because "fair" Portia is fundamentally "counterfeit" in her authority to pass judgment on Shylock; and when she does judge him, she does not do so fairly, according to an impartial interpretation of the law. Portia's deceptiveness, in her disguise as Balthasar, complements and ultimately reveals Bassanio's deceptiveness, which he had initially camouflaged behind the "golden" words: "So may the outward shows be least themselves. / The world is still deceived with ornament" (3.2.73-74).

Bassanio's relationship with Portia reflects a self-contradictory ambiguity that is both guileless and calculating at the same time. Bassanio can be described as sincerely insincere, generously self-serving or by any number of oxymora that reflect a type of ironic truth that is both true and false simultaneously. The truth is turned upside-down and inside-out, such that the truth appears to be simple and obvious, which it is not. This ambiguity has no explanation from within the perspective of the Christian/Jewish interpretive paradigm. That Bassanio is a devious fortune hunter contradicts the grand themes of the Christian/Jewish interpretive paradigm, which contrasts Shylock's materialism and greed with everyone else's love and generosity. The character of Bassanio makes sense only from the perspective of the honor/irony paradigm, which expects him to be both deceptive and money hungry—and no less attractive to Portia for that fact.

Identical opposites

The Merchant of Venice follows the general pattern set by Roman festive comedy: it inverts the values of normative reality. However, Shakespeare extends the logic of Roman comedy's irony to a point of absurdity, inverting normative *perception* of reality along with the festive inversion of conventional values, stretching what otherwise would have been crudely obvious to a point of subtle obscurity. Broad social parody for the lower classes (that is, a Roman-style comedy) thereby becomes least itself: ironic nuance for the sophisticated elite. While the festive irony of Roman comedy inverts the conventional values of Roman society, the inverse irony in *The Merchant of Venice* turns conventional perception of reality on its head.

Inverse irony, which begins with the premise that "the outward shows be *least* themselves [emphasis added]" (3.2.73), has several several corollaries:

- First, the truth is more complex than it appears; what may appear to be simple might mask something complex.
- Second, outward "show" is a certain indicator of falsehood.[119] What outwardly most appears to be true is that which is actually most false: reality is that which is least apparent, that which it least obviously appears to be.
- Third, superficial appearance and inner reality are opposite extremes.
- Fourth, extreme opposites can be easily confused for one another because they share a common outward appearance, even though one might presume that no two things could be more easily differentiated from one another than extreme opposites. In Antonio's example, both a "goodly apple" and an apple rotten at the core have the same shiny, red skin. Bassanio elaborates upon this point at length in his speech on appearances: he who looks like Hercules on the outside could be a coward on the inside; "fair orna-

ment" hides "grossness."

- Fifth, extreme opposites therefore can be easily substituted for one another without disrupting external appearances.
- Sixth, inverse opposites can likewise be reversed while appearing the same, just as a double negative is equal to a positive.
- And finally, language itself is fundamentally superficial and therefore misleading. Words of flattery and solemn promises can sound thoroughly convincing, yet in fact be quite false. Poetry and rhetoric can be powerfully persuasive, yet also be misleading: "what plea so tainted and corrupt / But, being seasoned with a gracious voice, / Obscures the show of evil? (3.2.75-77).

The festive logic of inverse irony, applied to the interpretation of *The Merchant of Venice*, reframes the meaning of the play. According to this perspective, Christian/Jewish themes that seem self-evident and obvious are in fact illusory and false; their purpose is to divert attention from issues of honor and irony.

- Portia's plea for Christian mercy masks a self-serving rationale for festive Roman immorality, which is antithetical to Christian morality. Festive self-indulgence disguises itself as Christian religiosity. Christian mercy appears to be a dominant thematic issue, even though personal honor—the sanctity of a bond—is more important to the play's meaning.
- Shylock's claim to a pound of flesh appears to be a demand for Old Testament-style retribution, but this perspective obscures the relevance of Roman law, which in some ways is antithetical to Jewish law. Ancient Roman law and ancient Roman honor are more relevant to the play's meaning than Jewish law and supposedly Jewish cruelty and vengefulness.
- Bassanio's romanticized appearance clouds the issue of personal honor, just as his poetic speech on sincerity and

love covers up his prosaic financial self-interest. Issues of personal honor—the sanctity of a promise and fidelity to the marital bond—are more important to the meaning of the play than whether the villain Shylock will spoil the happiness of Bassanio's idyllic love.

In sum, the issue of appearance and reality only appears to be simple in *The Merchant of Venice*, when in fact it is complex. The meaning of the play appears to be obvious, although its meaning is precisely that which at first does not appear to be obvious. The play that appears to be Christian apologetics is an illusion that masks a Roman-style festive comedy, which celebrates values that are antithetical to Christian morality.

At this point, it is fair to question the plausibility of this approach. Is it really possible to mistake something for its extreme opposite: Christian morality for Roman festivity, Jewish money lender for noble Roman, sincere love for calculated gold-digging? Is it possible to mask something as its antithesis? And more to the point: is it conceivable that Shakespeare could be playing games with these issues, hiding the meaning of *The Merchant of Venice* behind a veil of seemingly obvious-but-misleading themes? The credibility of the honor/irony approach to the play depends upon an affirmative answer to these questions.

While these complex issues have already been discussed at length, a fairly self-contained example within the play can prove the validity of the more general principle for the play as a whole. If it could be proven in a specific instance—in microcosm—that Shakespeare executes a literary sleight of hand to mask an example of the coarse bawdiness of Roman comedy behind a deceptive veil of lofty Christian spirituality, then it is not unreasonable to extrapolate that Shakespeare could have done something similar—in macrocosm—for the entire play: namely, to write a Roman-style comedy that hides festive immorality behind the spiritual-sounding verbiage of Christian morality. The case for inverse irony depends upon the misperception of that which would seem most impossible to misperceive: moral values that are self-evidently the most extreme opposites possible—sin and salvation, lust and chastity, party and prayer. So then it is fair to ask: can Shakespeare disguise salacious sexuality such that it could be mistaken for Christian morality? Could Shakespeare have hidden crude, carnal lust behind a veil of sublime Christian spirituality? Could anyone actually be deceived into confusing Christian morality for Roman carnival immorality?

In fact, Shakespeare has achieved this feat with surprising facility and enduring effectiveness—so enduring, in fact, that the double entendre uncovered here apparently has never been noted in any previously published research. The conversation between Jessica and Lorenzo that closes the play's third act is rife with the play's most vulgar bawdiness, but to date virtually all commentators have seen in it *only* the superficial appearance of spirituality and have failed entirely to notice—much less to find any meaning in—the flagrant sexual double entendre within it.

Jessica and Lorenzo are bantering with one another. They are trading clever remarks and witty come-backs, and in this spirit, they gossip about a friend. "And now, good sweet, say thy opinion," Lorenzo says. "How dost thou like the Lord Bassanio's wife?" (3.5.66-67). To which Jessica replies:

> Past all expressing. It is very meet
> The Lord Bassanio live an upright life,
> For, having such a blessing in his lady,
> He finds the joys of heaven here on earth,
> And if on earth he do not meane it,
> In reason he should never come to heaven.
> Why, if two gods should play some heavenly match
> And on the wager lay two earthly women,
> And Portia one: there must be something else[120]
> Pawned with the other, for the poor rude world
> Hath not her fellow. (3.5.68-78)

Line 71 here retains the word "meane," which was used in the Quarto, Folio and all other editions of *The Merchant of Venice* prior to the publication of the Alexander Pope edition in 1723.[121] Pope's edition was the first to substitute the word "merit," but most subsequent editions—*The New Variorum Edition* cites nine prior to 1892—have accepted Pope's emendation, as have virtually all recent editions. With the original word, "meane," the line can be understood as: if on earth he does not "intend" it; or, if on earth he does not have the means or capability to do it. This change in the original text is worth noting because substituting the word "merit" for "meane" distorts the meaning of the passage.

It has been universally assumed that in this passage, Jessica and Lorenzo are discussing matters of Christian spirituality; therefore, it is understandable that editors emend the text with the word "merit," which is commonly inserted here. It reinforces the passage's commonly-understood meaning, having to do with matters of religion and philosophy. Jessica and Lorenzo's dialogue "will go on to describe most explicitly the doctrine of divine harmony," according to one of the play's most distinguished contemporary interpreters.[122] "There is a delicacy here that is missing from Graziano's capering," Professor Lawrence Danson says.[123] But despite repeated references to "heaven" in this passage, there isn't anything particularly delicate about bawdy double entendre. Jessica's answer to the question "How dost thou like the Lord Bassanio's wife?" (3.5.67) is in fact an extended passage of double entendre in which she states quite clearly her opinion that Portia will be an incomparable sex partner for Bassanio.

First of all, it is strange that Jessica would introduce the topic of Christian morality by citing a pagan example of "two gods" playing "a heavenly match." Second, it is even more strange that Jessica would begin to elaborate upon Portia's saintliness by citing the example of two gods who "lay two earthly women" (3.5.74-75) on a wager. The double entendre here makes sense within the honor/irony paradigm, but has no evident purpose within the Christian/Jewish paradigm. Starting from the non-Christian premise of "*two* gods" is not a logical path to a conclusion that celebrates Christian morality; however, the premise of two gods who would "lay two earthly women" is comfortably within the purview of pagan Roman mythology.

Paradigms nothwithstanding, Jessica continues to speak in heavy double entendre throughout this passage, alluding directly to the pleasures of the flesh—erection, intercourse and orgasm. She says "it is very meet" that Bassanio should live an "upright life" in order to have "a blessing in his lady" and "come to heaven." And she speaks of "heaven here on earth." On the surface, she uses religious terminology, but only as a euphemism for Portia's alleged sexual expertise. In fact, Jessica fails to mention any spiritual aspect of Portia's personality whatever. She characterizes Portia entirely in terms of carnal pleasure.

Lorenzo comments on Jessica's opinion that Portia is an unrivaled sex partner, saying: "Even such a husband/ Hast thou of me as she is for a wife" (3.5.78-79). To which Jessica replies brightly, "Nay, but ask my opinion too of that." This exchange makes perfect sense if they are speaking bawdily, but this type of banter just doesn't ring true if they are speaking of religious or spiritual matters. It would be somewhat incongruous for Lorenzo to assert so quickly that his spiritual attainment is equal or better than Portia's, as if spiritual attainment were something for which highly religious people claimed bragging rights. And it would also be somewhat incongruous for Jessica to deny so quickly this claim, when she could be expected to revere the spirituality of her Christian husband, especially in contrast to the supposedly materialistic example of her Jewish father. However, it would be surprising if these characters had any interest in religious matters whatever, considering what we know about them at this point in the play: that Jessica has traded her late mother's ring for a monkey, and that Lorenzo cannot manage to keep a promised appointment time to rob his father-in-law's treasury. Clearly they are comic characters in the Plautine mold, not likely expositors of the Christian doctrine of divine harmony.

Critics working within the presumed Christian/Jewish interpretive paradigm—which is to say, all mainstream critics—are not predisposed to perceive any bawdy double entendre in this passage.[124] Furness' comprehensive (in 1892) summary of commentary in the New Variorum Edition of *The Merchant of Venice* cites ten scholars on the meaning of these lines; none of these pre-1892 scholars perceived anything remotely bawdy in Jessica's remarks. Neither is this passage in any way noted in E.A.M. Colman's *The Dramatic Use of Bawdy in Shakespeare*, even though Colman discusses many lesser and more doubtful instances of bawdy in the play.[125] A bawdy reading of this passage simply has no meaning in the context of a Christian/Jewish interpretation. Nevertheless, a purely non-bawdy take on these lines fails to explain why Shakespeare would want to cloak a Christian spiritual message in terms that could be interpreted as pagan and carnal. Why would Jessica speak of two gods in order to explain what is presumably a Christian perspective on heaven? And if it is Jessica's purpose is to discuss "lofty thoughts of love," as Danson says,[126] then why does Shakespeare have her do so in double entendre that could be understood as crudely sexual? Carnality masked as spirituality makes sense in an honor/irony paradigm, but spirituality masked as carnality has no meaning in a Christian/Jewish paradigm. Lewd double entendre fits the pattern defined by the honor/irony interpretive paradigm, which celebrates pagan immorality as integral to the Roman festive spirit, and postulates that vice hides behind what appears to be virtue, "hiding the grossness with fair ornament" (3.2.80), as Bassanio had said. But although the bawdiness is unquestionably present in Jessica's comment, it cannot be explained within the Christian/Jewish interpretive paradigm.

Most textual editors since Alexander Pope have gone so far as to change the original wording of this passage to an alternate wording that more strongly supports a purely spiritual, non-bawdy interpretation.[127] The substitution of the word "merit" for "meane" (3.5.72) enhances the notion of heaven as a reward for merit, while the retention of the word "meane" has no obvious meaning in the context of presumed Christian spirituality. This word replacement, which first appeared nearly 125 years after the first published editions of the play, is justified primarily by the belief that the passage—which is presumed to have a purely theological meaning—would be clearer if its words more closely matched its presumed meaning. Inserting the word "merit" confirms the preconceived notion that the passage should be understood theologically and also limits the passage to that interpretation. However, in stating that the line makes no sense without a word change, proponents of a religious reading of the passage concede that, in effect, the original text does not support their interpretation without emendation.

Wright and LaMar, in the editors' notes on this line in the popular Folger Shakespeare Library edition of the play, call this word change "an obvious improvement in sense."[128] Mahood, in her editor's notes on the line, says the passage:

> makes no sense...[without] Pope's brilliant emendation [which] is generally accepted.... the 'it' Bassanio has to show he deserves, if he is to be admitted to heaven, is the temporal blessing of having Portia for a wife.[129]

This emendation, however, diverts the focus of Jessica's remarks away from the question that she is supposedly answering. It is a *non sequitur* to answer a question about Portia's character with advice for Bassanio's salvation. The religious reading of this passage fails to explain what "Bassanio has to show he deserves, if he is to be admitted to heaven" has got to do with answering the question "What dost thou think of Lord Bassanio's wife?" (3.5.67). On the other hand, it is also a *non sequitur* to conclude that Portia "hath not her fellow" (3.5.78) from the premise that Bassanio should live a morally "upright life" (3.5.69). However, a bawdy reading of this passage says something plain and simple about Portia—that she is a sex partner without peer.

The bantering that leads into Jessica's description of Portia both supports the bawdy interpretation of these lines and suggests that a verbal sleight of hand is coming, that words can be used to deceive. In context, Jessica and Lorenzo are speaking playfully, teasing one another and having fun; they are not likely to be discussing religion and morality. After Lancelot Gobbo, the fool, has indulged in his sophomoric punning, Lorenzo says:

> The fool [Lancelot Gobbo] hath planted in his memory
> An army of good words, and I do know
> A many fools that stand in better place,
> Garnished like him, that for a tricksy word
> Defy the matter: (3.5.61-65)

Lorenzo's statement is a comment on Gobbo's punning; his next statement—that he knows many fools of higher standing that "for a tricksy word/ Defy the matter" clearly leads in to—and sets up—Jessica's bawdy double entendre: he is giving her the challenge to "defy the matter" with a "tricksy word"—a challenge that in fact she takes up. She follows Gobbo's example and succeeds magnificently in this challenge to "defy the matter" with a "tricksy word," using words in a manner that runs contrary to the superficial meaning normally expected. What she thinks of Portia is, she says, "past all expressing" (3.5.68), that is to say, somewhat beyond the normal bounds of polite speech; therefore she alludes to raw sex by appropriating religious terms for her intent. To see only religious content in what she says is to be among those who "stand in better place," but "defy the matter" because of a "tricksy word."

Jessica's ability to mask crude carnality behind the rhetoric of religion validates Bassanio's statement that "there is no vice so simple, but assumes/ Some mark of virtue on his outward parts" (3.2.81-82). "In religion," Bassanio had said, "What damned error but some sober brow/ Will bless it, and approve it with a text, / Hiding the grossness with fair ornament?" (3.2.77-80). Her spiritual-sounding salaciousness also validates Antonio's statement:

> The devil can cite Scripture for his purpose.
> An evil soul producing holy witness
> Is like a villain with a smiling cheek,
> A goodly apple rotten at the heart.
> O, what a goodly outside falsehood hath! (1.3.95-99)

To return to the questions raised previously: Is it really possible to mistake something for its extreme opposite—lust for holiness, greed for generosity, Roman comedy for Christian apologetics, ancient Roman for Jew? And is it conceivable that Shakespeare is using words to play games with these issues—and with his audience? In light of Jessica's bawdy comments about Portia, the answer to these questions is a definite "yes." The way Shakespeare melds together carnality and spirituality, hiding the former behind the mask of the latter, is the specific example that proves the more general point about inverse irony and the deceptiveness of superficial appearance to the interpretation of the play.

It is not incidental to the meaning of the play that Shakespeare plays games with words in this way. On the contrary, Jessica's word play exemplifies in microcosm the play's larger themes: that perception is a function of perceptual para-

digm, which shapes the basic value judgments related to issues of honor and deception, festive irony and normative reality, perception and reality. People see what they expect to see,
because it is human nature to take only a superficial glance
and see a confirmation of a pre-conceived notion.

Part three

Shifting paradigms: daylight/moonlight

Pervasive, overpowering moonlight is the defining metaphor for act five, which resolves and clarifies the play's main themes. This metaphor highlights the deceptiveness of superficial appearance and the consequent inversions of appearance and reality, truth and lies, honor and deception, festive and quotidian values—issues that are at the heart of the honor/irony paradigm. Shakespeare nowhere in *The Merchant of Venice* uses the word "paradigm." But in act five, where the play's themes are summarized and explained, Portia expounds the *concept* of a paradigm, elucidating how a framework of perspective can define cognition and how a radical shift in perspective can reframe perceived reality into its own antithesis, opposite to that which it initially appeared to be.

Value judgments are not absolute, but are defined by context and perspective, as Portia explains: "Nothing is good, I see, without respect," she says, commenting that she thinks the music she hears that night in her house "sounds much sweeter than by day" (5.1.99-100).

> The crow doth sing as sweetly as the lark
> When neither is attended, and I think
> The nightingale, if she should sing by day
> When every goose is cackling, would be thought
> No better a musician than the wren.
> How many things by season, seasoned are
> To their right praise and true perfection!   (5.1.102-108)

Portia explains that value judgments are relative and vary according to perspective. In her reckoning, "the crow doth sing as sweetly as the lark" because the comparative value of both bird songs is relative to the perspective of the listener who perceives value. What is extraordinarily beautiful by the light of the moon might be revealed to be quite ordinary by the bright light of day. Beauty is not an absolute value; it is defined by the relative perspective of the perceiver.

To say that two things are "as different as night and day" reflects the commonplace assumption that no two things could be more easily differentiated from one another than extreme opposites. But even extreme opposites such as night and day are not absolute. They are also defined by the perspective of the perceiver, as Portia explains with her comments about the brightness of the moon. In act five, the moonlight is extremely bright, so bright in fact that it appears to be pale daylight. "This night methinks is but the daylight sick," Portia says. "It looks a little paler. 'Tis a day/ Such as the day is when the sun is hid" (5.1.124-26). Like the relative beauty of the crow and the lark, the same degree of light that is considered dark by day is also considered bright by night. The metaphor used to describe extreme opposites—"as different as day and night"—is itself relative to perspective.

When values are described as the sharpest possible extreme antitheses, they begin to converge on a self-contradictory point of common identity, where inverse opposites start to look confusingly alike: the deeper into the night one goes, the closer to daybreak one gets. This convergence of opposites arises from the fact that antitheses are more easily described relative to each other, rather than as a single extreme in the absolute. When Portia wishes to say how extremely bright the moon is, she in effect asserts that extreme opposites (night and day) appear to be identical: a very bright night appears identical to a very dark day.

Portia's transposition of the extreme brightness of night into the extreme darkness of day is, in effect, a reframing of conventional perception of reality into a festive, mirror image opposite: what she defines as "daylight sick" is actually night.

In this context, the moonlight represents a festive inversion of moral values; the bright moon eclipses the sober values of daylight. But in addition, the bright moonlight itself is perceived as daylight—the opposite to what it actually is. The moonlight therefore inverts conventional *perception* of morality. The bright moonlight, like a false paradigm, gives the illusion that man sees clearly when instead he sees falsely, that what appear to be daylight values are actually festive, moonlight values. It illustrates, in microcosm, how "the outward shows be least themselves" (3.2.73). It is a metaphor for the play itself, which appears to be as clear and obvious as daylight, even though it is as subtle and ironic as moonlight that deceptively appears to be as bright as day.

Bassanio understands this topsy-turvy world of festive inversions, paradigm shifts and subtle irony. When he arrives at Belmont in a scene bleached white by the bright moonlight, he says: "We should hold day with the Antipodes, / If you [Portia] would walk in absence of the sun" (5.1.127-128). The "absence of the sun" is an inverse way of saying "night." To "hold day with the Antipodes" is Bassanio's paradigm shift, his way of calling the bright night "daylight sick." Like Portia, he has found a way to say that extreme opposites can function as equivalents, and be confused for one another, relative to perspective.

When Portia first arrives on the scene in act five, she uses the relative brightness of light as a metaphor for man's ability to perceive moral value and to make moral value judgments. "That light we see is burning in my hall," Portia says: "How far that little candle throws his beams— / So shines a good deed in a naughty world" (5.1.89-91). However, in this case, the moonlight blots out the candle light, which cannot be seen.

Nerissa: When the moon shone, we did not see the candle.
Portia: So doth the greater glory dim the less.
A substitute shines brightly as a king

Until a king be by, and then his state
Empties itself, as doth an inland brook
Into the main of waters: (5.1.92-97).

According to one framework of perspective, the candle shines brightly: "How far that little candle throws his beams—" (5.1.90). But judged according to an alternate perspective, the same candle is too dim to be seen: "When the moon shone, we did not see the candle" (5.1.92). In a non-festive context, the sun would be considered the greater light, as compared to the moon; but in these festive circumstances, the moon is the greater light, overwhelming the brightness of the candle.

A candle is a religious symbol that symbolizes God's light. In the New Testament, Jesus uses a candlelight as a metaphor for His message. "Ye are the light of the world. A city that is set on a hill cannot be hid. Neither do ye light a candle and put it under a bushel, but on a candlestick; and it gives light unto all that are in the house," Jesus says. "Let your light shine so before me, that all may see your good works" (Matt. 5:14-16). Danson says that:

It is no accident that the portion of Scripture to which Portia alludes in her talk about brightly shining candles immediately precedes Christ's words about his relationship to that covenant: 'Thinke not that I am come to destroye the Law, or the Prophetes. I am not come to destroye them, but to fulfil them.'[130]

However, moonlight is commonly a metaphor for festive values, as when the lying, stealing, drunkenly self-indulgent Sir John Falstaff describes himself and his cohorts as "Diana's foresters, gentlemen of the shade, minions of the moon" (*Henry IV, Part 1,* I.ii.29-30). "We that take purses go by the moon and the seven stars, and not by Phoebus," Falstaff says (I.ii.14-15). In a non-festive frame of reference, the bright light of a candle stands out in the darkness: "How far that little candle throws his beams— / So shines a good deed in a naughty world" (5.1.89-91), as Portia had said. But the "naughty world" Portia refers to is the world of festive immorality, the "naughty times/

[that] Put bars between the owners and their rights" (3.2.18-19). And in *The Merchant of Venice*, the "naughty" night world predominates over the conventional morality of daylight.

Act five of *The Merchant of Venice* begins with an extended discussion of how bright the moonlight is. "The moon shines bright," Lorenzo says (5.1.1), initiating a dialogue with Jessica in which they exchange the phrase "in such a night" no less than seven times before they are interrupted by a messenger. As soon as the messenger leaves, Lorenzo begins again: "How sweet the moonlight sleeps upon this bank!" (5.1.54). When musicians interrupt his reverie, he says: "Come, ho! and wake Diana with a hymn" (5.1.66), referring to the Roman goddess of chastity, hunting and the moon. In such a night, Lorenzo says, Troilus longed for Cressida. "In such a night," Jessica replies, "Did Thisbe fearfully o'ertrip the dew/ And saw the lion's shadow ere himself, / And ran dismayed away" (5.1.6-9). In such a night, Lorenzo counters, Dido longed for her love. In such a night, Jessica answers, Medea gathered herbs (5.1.9-13). "In such a night," says Lorenzo:

> Did Jessica steal from the wealthy Jew
> And with an unthrift love did run from Venice
> As far as Belmont.
> **Jessica:** In such a night
> Did young Lorenzo swear he loved her well,
> Stealing her soul with many vows of faith
> And ne'er a true one.
> **Lorenzo:** In such a night
> Did pretty Jessica, like a little shrew,
> Slander her love, and he forgave it her.   (5.1.14-22)

The repetition of the phrase "in such a night" is a rhetorical device that serves several purposes. First, it emphasizes the fullness and brightness of the moon: "The moon shines bright" is the antecedent that defines what type of night Jessica and Lorenzo are discussing; when they reiterate: "in such a night," they mean: in a night such as this one, when the moon is shining so brightly. Second, the reiteration of the phrase "in such a night" identifies the bright moonlight with Jessica's escape from Shylock, an act that symbolizes, in microcosm, the play's festive rebellion against daylight values. The moon is nature's equivalent to society's festive day; it presides over the comic lunacy of emotions turned loose to run their course unrestrained; the fairies, the spirits of nature, are in command, effecting seemingly unnatural changes in daylight's laws of nature, as in *A Midsummer Night's Dream.*

Third, the dialogue "in such a night" frames Jessica's rebellion against Shylock in the context of classical, pagan literature—not anything in Jewish or Christian tradition. And fourth, this context defines the revolt against Shylock in terms of a continuum of classical precedent that is distinctly dishonorable. Sigurd Burckhardt, among others, has noted that the stories Jessica and Lorenzo call to mind are a "genealogy of fly-by-night love: betrayal (Troilus and Cressida), disaster (Pyramus and Thisbe), desertion (Dido and Aeneas), sorcery (Medea), and theft (Jessica)."[151] Similarly, R. Chris Hassell, Jr. notes:

> The lovers recall past romantic figures, all of whom—Cressid, Thisbe, Dido, and Medea—connote tragedy and perversion: fickleness, familial discord, unfaithfulness and murder.[152]

Danson also takes note of the irony inherent to the examples of love cited by Jessica and Lorenzo. The rebellion against daylight values (in microcosm, Jessica's rebellion against Shylock) is defined in a context of classical dishonor, rather than in terms of conflicting Christian and Jewish morality.

Finally, the dialogue "in such a night" places Lorenzo squarely in that classical tradition of dishonorable love: Jessica accuses Lorenzo of false vows of faith, swearing that "he loved her well...with many vows of faith, / And ne'er a true one" (5.1.17-19). This playful teasing is an example of "kidding on the level," to use Professor A.W. Nuttall's term."[133] Jessica may be teasing Lorenzo, but she simultaneously communicates an unpleasant truth: that Lorenzo has broken his promises—the promise to arrive for their rendezvous on time, for example.

When Portia confronts Bassanio about his missing ring, he attempts to re-establish his credibility by invoking "these blessed candles of the night" (5.1.220)—the same "blessed" candles that just previously were not bright enough to be seen by the even-brighter light of the festive moon. As Bassanio begs forgiveness, he promises yet again: "in the hearing of these many friends, / I swear to thee, even by thine own fair eyes, / Wherein I see myself—" (5.1.241-243). However, Portia interrupts him at this point:

> Mark you but that!
> In both my eyes he doubly sees himself,
> In each eye one. Swear by your double self,
> And there's an oath of credit.   (5.1.243-246)

In asking Bassanio to "swear" by his "double self," Portia focuses directly on one of the key issues of the play: the irony of Bassanio's claim to honor. Swearing by both eyes would be to make an absolute claim on the basis of a relative foundation—superficial appearance and human perception. Promises, she says, must be based on something more reliable than appearances, noting that it is contradictory to swear fidelity by invoking the eyes, a mirror image that is necessarily superficial and deceptive. However, she suggests that there are possible grounds for certainty in a self-contradictory, double ambiguity. "Swear by your double self," she says, suggesting that a double negative might equal a positive.

Portia's parables about perspective explain the festive inversions that are at the heart of the honor/irony approach to *The Merchant of Venice.* According to this interpretation, moral values such as "mercy" and "justice" are relative to interpretive paradigm. Justice is cruel from a festive perspective, but equitable from a non-festive perspective. Mercy is highly moral from a Christian religious perspective, but might be a travesty of Roman law. Extracting a pound of flesh is despicable from a Christian perspective, but admirable from a Roman perspective. And what appears to be as clear as day may actually be as illusory as moonlight haze. A single matter of fact might be perceived either as itself or its opposite, a perception that varies according to the framework of perspective.

Explicating *The Merchant of Venice* in terms of interpretive paradigms is ultimately self-reductive: it is not an approach that is foreign to the play, a Procrustean bed into which the play is artificially forced. On the contrary, understanding how perspective shapes meaning is a fundamental message of the play itself. The play several times makes the point that perspective defines perception. It is an issue that bears directly upon the play's focus on the deceptiveness of superficial appearance, which Bassanio expounds upon at length in act three and which Portia helps to explain in act five with her parables of larks and ravens, candles and moonlight. Act five, which resolves the plot as well as the play's themes, is an essential part of the play's festive irony and thematic exposition.

The symbolism of moonlight and candles has little or no evident meaning in the context of the Christian/Jewish interpretive paradigm. Neither moonlight nor candles have much to do with Christian/Jewish conflict generally nor with the clash of values between Antonio and Shylock in particular. Professor John Lyon, in his judicious summary of the issues raised by the play, frankly admits that critical opinion—which is, of course, based on the assumption of a Christian/Jewish interpretive paradigm—does not really understand why Portia discusses the philosophical issues that she raises in act five:

> Such speculation [on candles, etc.] has a teasingly elusive relation
> to the events of the play and to Portia's own actions, but a relation

more easily sensed than specified....

Such eloquence is curiously and seductively moving, but senten-tiousness, even as elegiacly accepting as this is, remains in a prob-lematic relation to the dramatic action. The words derive their mourn-ful authority from Portia's voice of experience, but our sense of the ways in which they refer to such past experiences remains hazy. The larger particularities of this play seem curiously to slip between the immediate and mundane incidentals which prompt Portia's musings—the candle in her own house, the overhearing of her own music—and the conceited elaborations which her thoughts receive. We might suspect that Portia's wisdom is in fact the dramatist's sleight of hand, and that what matters here is mood, not philosophy.[134]

In so many words, Lyon says that it's not clear how to inte-grate the symbolism and imagery of act five into the meaning of the play, as it's generally understood. The conflict between Antonio and Shylock is resolved in act four; therefore, the play's thematic issues are presumed to have been resolved in act four—and all of act five is deemed to be thematically a point off the curve. That act five's themes do not jibe with the cus-tomary themes of the Christian/Jewish paradigm Lyon sees as a weakness of the play, rather than as a shortcoming of interpretative paradigm.

The perceived thematic dissonance between act five and the rest of the play has also prompted some to conclude that the dramatic structure of the play is also something of an anomaly: the play's final act is often considered more of a postscript to the play than a summary and resolution, as the final act would be in other Shakespeare plays. Professor Robert Ornstein speaks for many when he states that, unlike most Shakespearean comedies, which:

achieve their dramatic resolutions...[at] very near the end of their concluding scenes, *The Merchant* and *A Dream* have a somewhat different dramatic structure. Their climactic moments of conflict occur in their fourth and third acts respectively, and all antagonism and discord are resolved before their fourth and fifth acts begin. In both plays the last act is a long graceful coda in which the triumph of love is celebrated by a dramatic entertainment or charade, with witty gives and affectionate teasings, with music and poetry.[135]

From the perspective of the honor/irony paradigm, however, act five is directly on target as a summary and resolution of themes raised earlier in the play. The issues of moonlight, morality and shifting perceptual paradigms are greatly relevant to the fundamental themes of the honor/irony interpretation: appearance and reality, truth and lies, honor and deception. Act five is rich with thematic material relevant to both the Portia/Bassanio plot stream and the Antonio/Shylock subplot. The resolution of the wedding ring deceit emphasizes the importance of keeping a promise—that a man's word is his bond—which is crucial to the ideal of ancient Roman honor. When the play is interpreted from the perspective of the honor/irony paradigm, act five fully conforms to the structural pattern defined by Shakespeare's other comedies, in which the themes are resolved in the final act. *The Merchant of Venice* is an exception to the structural pattern defined by Shakespeare's other comedies only when it is interpreted in terms of themes derived from a Christian/Jewish paradigm.

Absolute values in a relative world

The principle that value judgments are relative to perspective reflects a fundamental assumption of festive comedy: that context defines meaning. A single action could either be condemned as immoral in a non-festive context or celebrated as great entertainment in a festive context: a single statement could be either despicable or humorous, depending upon the interpretive perspective. For example, according to the festive values of Roman comedy, mercy is considered good and usury is considered bad; while according to the normative perspective of ancient Rome, enforcement of the law is considered noble, while putting aside the law for the sake of mercy is considered to be a spineless compromise. The basic facts remain the same, but can be interpreted antithetically, according to complementary-but-inverse frames of reference within the ancient Roman cultural paradigm. Festive comedy's humor depends upon the audience's ability to make a mental comparison between comic extravagance and quotidian restraint and to recognize the irony in former's inversion of the latter's standards.

The flexibility of perspective inherent to comedy is antithetical to the rigidity of perspective that is characteristic of the ideal of ancient Roman honor. Ancient Roman honor is a nontheistic absolute that enables a man to establish for himself an unchanging standard of personal integrity in a modern world of relative standards and moral compromise. The man of ancient Roman honor remains constant, even though truth itself appears to be variable and relative. In contrast to virtually all of his contemporaries, he remains constant in his personal commitment to an unchanging morality of absolutes in a world of constantly changing appearances and misleading perceptions. As a Renaissance ideal, the man of ancient Roman honor represents a moral alternative to contemporary society, in which false promises and unstable commitments predominate, where the truth and what outwardly appears to be true might be as different as night and day. In this environment, the man of ancient Roman honor is an island of reliability in a sea of uncertainty, a lonely beacon of light who cannot be recognized because of the overpowering brightness of the moon. He alone can be trusted to keep his promises, to be consistent in word and deed, appearance and reality. He represents an absolute ideal in a relative world.

In *As You Like It*, Orlando speaks of "the constant service of the antique world" (II.iii.57). The unshakable commitment to remain "constant"—rigidly committed to an absolute ideal— is a fundamental attribute that differentiates the noble individual from the fickle mob.[136] In *Julius Caesar*, Portia says: "O constancy, be strong upon my side; / Set a mountain 'tween my heart and tongue!" (II.iv.6-7). When Portia mutilates her thigh, she tells Brutus that she had done so as "strong proof of my constancy" (*JC*, II.i.299). Plutarch's version of this incident uses similar wording:

> How may I show my duty towards thee, and how much I would do for thy sake, if I cannot constantly bear a secret mischance or grief with thee, which requireth secrecy and fidelity?[137]

Coriolanus also asserts that he is "constant." When Cominus reminds him that "it is your former promise" to fight in another military campaign, he replies: "Sir, it is; / And I am constant" (*Cor.*, I.i.242-244).

Like Coriolanus, Julius Caesar identifies himself as someone who is constant, comparing himself to the North Star, the pole star, which alone among the many stars in the sky appears to remain unmoved in its place—an absolute value in a relative world. He declines to accede to repeated pleas that he show mercy and repeal his decision to banish Cimber because his commitment to constancy demands that he be inflexible on principle:

> I could be well moved, if I were as you;
> If I could pray to move, prayers would move me;
> But I am constant as the Northern Star,
> Of whose true-fixed and resting quality
> There is no fellow in the firmament.
> The skies are painted with unnumb'red sparks,
> They are all fire and every one doth shine;
> There's but one in all doth hold his place.
> So in the world; 'tis furnished well with men,
> And men are flesh and blood, and apprehensive,
> Yet in the number I do know but one
> That unassailable holds on his rank,
> Unshaked of motion; and that I am he,
> Let me a little show it, even in this—
> That I was constant Cimber should be banished,
> And constant do remain to keep him so.   (III.i.58-73)

The last statement Caesar makes before his death, the pivotal moment at the centerpoint of the play that (like Bassanio's speech on outward shows in act three) brings the play's themes into focus is this defiant resolution to remain constant. Caesar's refusal to yield to the pleading that he be more lenient to Cimber was not in itself the reason for his assassination, but it is the defining gesture that immediately precipitates his murder. What could be called Caesar's last stand is a symbolic defense of constancy—as well as a final stand against mercy or clemency of any kind, which would compromise his constancy.[138]

In contradistinction to Caesar, Othello falls victim to his fate because he is not constant. "These Moors are changeable in their wills," Iago says to Roderigo. "The food that to him now is as luscious as locusts, shall be to him shortly as little as coloquintida" (*Oth.*, I.iii.352-355). Iago knows that because Othello is not constant, he can be manipulated by deceptive external appearances and brought down. Desdemona, in contrast (though accused of infidelity) remains constant, notably in her commitment to all her vows, including her promise to Cassio to persist in advocating his cause to Othello.

While the man of honor is committed to an absolute, unchanging concept of honor, comedy favors compromise, relative values and inverted hierarchies. Leniency and mercy are considered to be correct and noble in the context of comedy; Portia's plea for mercy in *The Merchant of Venice* is ostensibly the nobler moral alternative for Shylock. But in the context of everyday life in Rome (or within a tragic drama, such as *Julius Caesar*), the call for mercy is antithetical to nobility, which must remain constant even in the face of a popular outcry for mercy.

In *The Merchant of Venice*, the word "constant" is used only twice. Lorenzo uses the word to describe his relationship to Jessica, saying that she shall "be placed in my constant soul" (2.6.57). He does not hesitate to speak of his "constant soul" even though there's no particular evidence of it anywhere. Jessica says he has made "many vows of faith, / And ne'er a true one" (5.1.18-19). Portia also uses the word "constant." When Bassanio learns that Antonio will not be able to meet the terms of his bond with Shylock, Portia says:

> There are some shrewd contents in yond same paper
> That steals the colour from Bassanio's cheek.
> Some dear friend dead, else nothing in the world
> Could turn so much the constitution
> Of any constant man...   (3.2.241-245)

Bassanio, of course, proves himself to be less than "constant" in several ways. Shylock, on the other hand, finds himself in conflict with the rest of Venice precisely because he remains constant in his insistence upon the terms of his bond with Antonio.

A great deal has been written about *The Merchant of Venice* in regard to Jewish and Christian laws regulating usury. However, in the context of the ideal of ancient Roman honor, "usury" has a different meaning, as an incident from the life of Coriolanus makes clear. In *Coriolanus*, usury is among the alleged injustices for which the lower class resents the aristocratic power elite. In the opening scenes of the play, the rabble is agitating about the price of corn; the people are ready to rebel against a Roman government that makes "edicts for usury, to support usurers" (I.i.83-84). In contradistinction to the crowd, Coriolanus favors enforcement of the laws of usury and opposes any concession to the demands of the people. Like Caesar, he refuses to compromise on principle because, in his view, any compromise (even on the usury laws) would be a deviation from his unswerving commitment to constancy. For that reason, the plebeians identify Coriolanus, Shakespeare's most resolute champion of Roman nobility, as "the chief enemy to the people" (I.i.7) and "a very dog to the commonalty" (I.i.28-29).

Plutarch clarifies these issues in his biography of Coriolanus:

> It fortuned there grew sedition in the city, because the Senate did favour the rich against the people, who did complain of the sore oppression of usurers, of whom they borrowed money. For those that had little, were yet spoiled of that little they had by their creditors, for lack of ability to pay the usury: who offered their goods to be sold to them that would give most. And such as had nothing left, their bodies were laid hold of, and they were made their bondmen, notwithstanding all the wounds and cuts they showed, which they had received in many battles, fighting for the defense of their country and commonwealth: of the which, the last war they made was against the Sabynes, wherein they fought upon the promise the rich men had made them, that from thenceforth they would entreat them more gently, and also upon the word of Marcus Valerius chief of the Senate, who by authority of the Council, and in the behalf of the rich, said they should perform that they had promised. But after that they had faithfully served in this last battle of all, where they overcame their enemies, seeing they were never a whit the better, nor more gently entreated, and that the Senate would give no ear to them, but made as though they had forgotten their former promise, and suffered them to be made slaves and bondmen to their creditors, and besides, to be turned out of all that ever they had: they fell then even to flat rebellion and mutine, and to stir up dangerous tumults within the city..... For some thought it was reason, they should somewhat yield to the poor people's request, and that they should a little qualify the severity of the law. Others held hard against that opinion, and that was Martius [that is, Coriolanus] for one. For he alleged, that the creditors, losing their money they had lent, was not the worst thing that was thereby: but that the lenity that was favoured, was a beginning of disobedience, and that the proud attempt of the communalty, was to abolish law, and to bring all to confusion. Therefore, he said, if the Senate were wise, they should betimes prevent and quench this ill-favoured and worse meant beginning.[139]

Coriolanus favors the law; he opposes confusion. He is inflexible on these principles and blind to any other possible considerations. Coriolanus justifies usury on the basis of his unwavering commitment to the law and all that the law stands for—a commitment that remains constant and uncompromising, despite the threat of an insurrection by the lower classes, even though Plutarch's account concedes that the people had a valid complaint with the upper class, which had not kept the promises it had made to them prior to the war. Coriolanus, then, was against any compromise on the enforcement of the laws of usury for the sake of the plebeians, "notwithstanding all the wounds and cuts they showed" from their military service, even though he himself did not want to show his wounds in public, as he was expected to do in order to win election to the political post he was seeking.

Coriolanus' stand against the crowd's plea for relief from usury is a principled resolve similar to Caesar's refusal to respond to the call for mercy on behalf of Cimber. To him, principle is more important than people and their happiness. His murderous rancor against the people is far harsher than Shylock's demand for a pound of flesh:

> Hang 'em. They say!...
> Would the nobility lay aside their ruth
> And let me use my sword, I'd make a quarry
> With thousands of these quarter'd slaves as high
> As I could pick my lance.   (I.i.194-204)

Despite Coriolanus' openly-stated desire to personally slaughter thousands of his fellow Romans, Shakespeare leaves no doubt that he is a man of honor, whose contempt for the people is ultimately justified by the fate that he suffers at their hands. He may not be kind, humane or merciful, but nonetheless, he is to be admired for his nobility, which remains constant.

Critics may or may not be sympathetic to Shylock, but generally (with the example of Coriolanus as a notable exception) no one defends usury, which has never been a popular cause. However, neither Coriolanus nor Shylock are intended to be crowd-pleasing characters; their principles are in conflict with popular opinion. Both Coriolanus and Shylock can be considered exemplars of ancient Roman honor because they remain constant in their stand for law—even when the law is as unpopular as the laws of usury. One can imagine Coriolanus saying with Shylock: "I stand here for law" (*MV*, 4.1.141).

Honor/isolation

Shakespeare's conception of Roman honor, shaped by his reading of Plutarch, assumes the inevitability of conflict between contrary poles of humanity: the noble individual, who remains unmoved despite all, and the ignoble crowd, which is volatile, unpredictable and constantly changing.[140] In contradistinction to a principled constancy that would defend even usury, the people easily yield to unruly emotion and quickly reverse their judgments. They are manipulated by powerful rhetoric and deceived by superficial appearance. An agitated mob can be turned around suddenly, completely reversing its course of action without even realizing that it has changed direction and without losing a bit of its initial emotional intensity.

In *Julius Caesar,* Brutus speaks to the plebeians in order to justify Caesar's assassination, asking if anyone disagrees with him. In response, the people shout as one man: "None, Brutus, none!" (*JC*, III.ii.36). They agree with him completely and are wildly with enthusiastic in their support for what he has done:

> **First Plebeian**: Bring him [Brutus] with triumph home unto his house.
> **Second Plebeian**: Give him a statue with his ancestors.
> **Third Plebeian**: Let him be Caesar.
> **Fourth Plebeian**: Caesar's better parts
> Shall be crowned in Brutus.
> **First Plebeian**: We'll bring him to his house with shouts and clamors.
> (III.ii.49-54)

Just a few short minutes later, this same crowd is equally impassioned against Brutus. In a heartbeat, the people completely reverse their opinion of Brutus—a reversal of fortune as extreme and sudden as Shylock's comic reversal of fortune in Portia's court:

Second Plebeian: O noble Caesar!
Third Plebeian: O woeful day!
Fourth Plebeian: O traitors, villains! [meaning Brutus and his fellow conspirators]
First Plebeian: O most bloody sight!
Second Plebeian: We will be revenged.
All: Revenge! About! Seek! Burn! Fire! Kill! Slay! Let not a traitor live!
(III.ii.201-207)

The very same plebeian who had wanted to bring Brutus "with triumph home unto his house" (III.ii.49-50) is the individual who shortly afterward cries out "We'll burn the house of Brutus" (III.ii.233). All are swept away by the emotion of the moment, aroused by the rhetoric of Antony's speech beginning: "Friends, Romans, countrymen, lend me your ears; / I have come to bury Caesar, not to praise him" (III.ii.75-76).

In contrast to the crowd, which is easily agitated by Antony's rhetoric, Caesar himself was impervious to the power of words, which are superficial and inconstant—and Caesar above all is constant. Caesar pointedly states that he will not be seduced by the sweet talk of flattery:

Be not fond to think that Caesar bears such rebel blood[141]
That will be thawed from the true quality
With that which melteth fools—I mean sweet words,
Low-crooked curtsies, and base spaniel fawning.   (*JC*, III.i.39-43)

His contempt for ignoble "fawning" recalls the disdain in Shylock's comment: "How like a fawning publican he looks" (*MV*, 1.3.38).

The man of honor is constant: he remains impervious to flattery and he refuses to flatter others. The plebeians' susceptibility to flattery is one reason why Coriolanus hates them: if they can be moved by flattery, they are not constant. If they are not constant, they cannot be trusted. If they cannot be trusted, they lack honor and are therefore contemptible:

...He that trusts to you,
Where he should find you lions, finds you hares;

Where foxes, geese. You are no surer, no,
Than is the coal of fire upon the ice,
Or hailstone in the sun. Your virtue is
To make him worthy whose offence subdues him,
And curse that justice did it. Who deserves greatness
Deserves your hate; and your affections are
A sick man's appetite, who desires most that
Which would increase his evil. He that depends
Upon your favors swims with fins of lead
And hews down oaks with rushes. Hang ye! Trust ye?
With every minute you do change a mind,
And call him noble that was now your hate,
Him vile that was your garland.   (*Cor.*, I.i.174-188)

Coriolanus assumes, like Bassanio, that appearance does not correspond with reality, that words and deeds diverge. But unlike Bassanio, who utilizes this knowledge for his own advancement, Coriolanus condemns the great mass of men for this moral deficiency. In so far as fawning is concerned, the comic Bassanio has no problem manipulating words for his own advantage; in contrast, the tragic Coriolanus resolutely refuses to do so, as he makes clear right away, in his first scene in the play. To a citizen who cordially invites him to speak, saying "We have ever your good word," Coriolanus replies: "He that will give good words to thee will flatter / Beneath abhorring" (*Cor.*, I.i.171-172).

As events subsequently prove, Coriolanus' reluctance to flatter the people proves fatal to him. The people expected him to show evidence of his war wounds, dress humbly and profess his respect for them—but he balks at making any kind of outward show for them. He cannot show respect for people he does not respect, even though political expediency demands that he do so. He is reluctant to make any outward show of his need for the plebeians' political support; and they, in turn, not only decline to reward him for his military leadership by making him a consul, they banish him from Rome because of his refusal to make the expected superficial gestures. Coriolanus had refused to mask his contempt for the lower classes behind a show of respect; he had resisted the notion of humbling himself in any way before them.

The noble individual and the ignoble crowd, then, are antagonistic antipodes, as contrary as a "coal of fire upon the ice, / Or a hailstone in the sun" (*Cor.* I. I.78-79). Even prior to his banishment, Coriolanus' spiritual isolation defined a profound gulf between him and his fellow Romans. The vote against Coriolanus, in effect, ratifies his already deeply rooted alienation from the city and its inhabitants. His spiritual distance from his contemporaries is evident following the vote to banish him, when he alone remains unmoved, declining to make any outward show of emotion that would betray dependence in any way upon popular opinion. In contrast to his personal stoicism, both aristocrats and plebeians alike wear their emotions on their sleeves, so to speak. According to Plutarch:

> There needed no difference of garments I warrant you, nor outward shows to know a plebeian from a patrician, for they were easily discerned by their looks. For he that was on the people's side, looked cheerily on the matter: but he that was sad, and hung down his head, he was sure of the noblemen's side. Saving Martius [that is, Coriolanus] alone, who neither in his countenance nor in his gait, did ever show himself abashed, or once let fall his great courage: be he only of all other gentlemen that were angry at his fortune, did outwardly show no manner of passion, nor care at all of himself.[142]

"Shakespeare follows Plutarch so very closely that he often echoes the phraseology of the magnificent Elizabethan translation by Sir Thomas North," Harry Levin writes in his introduction to *Coriolanus*, noting that Volumina's speech to her son, Coriolanus, "eloquently massive as it is, is scarcely more than a metrical adaptation of North's prose.[143] However, the phraseology in the Plutarch passage quoted above, which speaks of "outward shows," is notable for its similarity to Bassanio's key speech in *The Merchant of Venice*: "So may the outward shows be least themselves." (3.2.73).

The plebeians judge Coriolanus on the basis of superficial

appearance; they vote against him because he refuses to make a hypocritical show of respect for them. The vote against him strictly follows class distinctions, with the aristocrats in favor of him, and the plebeians not. Plebeian justice—mobocracy— (though in a tragic context) is an inversion of the social order and its aristocratic values, analogous to the festive inversion of justice customary to Roman comedy.

Ironically, Coriolanus is exiled (and like Caesar, ultimately killed) precisely for that noble constancy for which he should have been respected. Like Shylock, he is condemned for his inflexible constancy, which runs against the grain of popular opinion. In the context of tragedy, which celebrates normative restraint, the man of ancient Roman honor is admired for his nobility; but in the context of comedy, which celebrates festive license, he is despised as a villainous fool. A common denominator to Shakespeare's tragedy and comedy is that in both tragedy and comedy, the noble man of constancy falls victim to the ignoble, constantly changing crowd.

Coriolanus' contentious personality makes explicit a contempt for the great majority of men that is inherent to the ideal of ancient Roman honor. This ideal is both elitist and retrogressive: it assumes that very few can hope to attain the moral stature attributed to Rome's founding fathers. The ancient Romans themselves lamented the ostensible moral deterioration of their own age in comparison to the nobility of their forefathers in Rome's earlier, golden age:

> The Romans had created an impossible ideal and transferred it to the past, making myths out of the men who were their forefathers. The Roman obsession with the greatness of their ancestors is epitomized in Cicero's well-known apostroph (Tusc. Disp.I.1): ... 'What people ever had such dignity, such stout-heartedness, greatness of spirit, uprightness, loyalty, such shining qualities of every kind that they could possibly compare with our ancestors?'
>
> The guiding principle for behavior was *mos maiorum*, our forefathers' precedent. But which forefathers? Cicero lavished praise on Cato's day, and Cato himself evokes the precedent of still earlier

maiores nostri. No Roman of any age could fulfill the dictates of *mos maiorum*...[144]

The ideal of ancient Roman honor is inherently elitist and retrogressive, then, because even in ancient times, the great majority of contemporary men were perceived to fall short of an ideal standard defined by individuals even more ancient than they. Relatively early in Rome's history, Coriolanus illuminates a gap between contemporary reality and ancient ideal; he is adamant against flattering the people, for whom he has great contempt. In contrast, Antony later built his career on flattery of his troops and the people, but the common denominator with Coriolanus is the failure of the great mass of men to remain constant and committed to the Roman ideal of honor.[145]

The gap between contemporary reality and ancient ideal increases proportionally to the historical distance between contemporary society and Rome's beginning. The man of ancient Roman honor is an extreme rarity at any time, in any place. He stands at a distance from general society, contemptuous of common people and hated in turn by them, like Coriolanus. But in the context of Renaissance Europe, which is separated from ancient Rome by the barriers of history and culture, the man of ancient Roman honor is, in effect, an atavistic anomaly, a moral anachronism. He is motivated by an ethos completely alien and incomprehensible to the masses, one that runs against the grain of modernity in sensibility and style. His contemporaries perceive him as a madman or a criminal, a pariah, an alien, an ignoble clown.

Shylock the Jew is Shakespeare's metaphor for the anachronism of a man of ancient Roman honor in the modern world. Shakespeare's point is that nobility is so rare as to be virtually non-existent in the modern world; and that an essentially shallow, morally insensitive society would have so little understanding of ancient Roman honor that it would be entirely unable to recognize an exemplar of that ideal. The moral obtuseness of modernity is presumed to be so great that modern men, who are overly impressed by superficial appearance, would fail to recognize the qualities of character and personality that are typical of nobility and honor. They would have disdain for the man of honor because he and his values are alien according to their perspective. The great mass of men are presumed to be so easily manipulated, morally blind and subject to superficial appearance that they cannot even distinguish the man of ancient Roman honor from his extreme antithesis, a Jewish money lender.

Shylock personifies the essential isolation of a man of ancient Roman honor in the modern world—the individual who alone remains constant in the midst of a constantly changing and compromising morally-obtuse majority—surrounded by people who have no sympathy or understanding whatever for his personal value system. Like Hamlet, he is spiritually isolated amid a fickle, uncomprehending majority that does not have a clue as to what makes him tick. He is in an intolerable existential situation: motivated by values entirely foreign to those around him, his thoughts and ideas separate him from his contemporaries to a point of isolation approaching solipsism. Shylock alone—in a world of facilely broken promises—is a man of constancy whose word is his bond; he is alone among those for whom word and deed are variable, for whom appearance and reality might be as different as night and day.

As a dramatic concept, the anachronism of an ancient Roman in modern society achieves a dual, contradictory purpose. On one hand, it increases the spiritual distance between this lonely, noble individual from the prevailing moral laxity of his ignoble contemporaries, sharpening the contrast between his personal dignity the superficial fecklessness of everyone else. On the other hand, the anachronism of an ancient Roman in modern society belittles the great man by placing him in a comic context that humorously deflates his dignity, subjecting him to humiliating and petty circumstances—because the modern age is necessarily diminished in grandeur in comparison to the glory of ancient times and therefore inherently more farcical than heroic.[146]

It makes perfect sense that a character personifying a rarely-attained ideal that runs contrary to popular opinion in modern Europe should be devised at a greatly ironic distance from the audience. It simply adds one more layer of metaphor to a play already believed to be rich with multiple levels of meaning. The concept of an intentionally cryptic Shakespeare hiding a noble Roman behind a comic mask does not in the least diminish *The Merchant of Venice*'s proven appeal at other levels.

Part four

Rome/Venice

The notion that ancient Roman honor could be alive and well in Renaissance Venice is a concept that is not unique to Shakespeare in *The Merchant of Venice*. It was not unusual for Protestant Englishmen in Shakespeare's day to identify modern Venice with ancient Rome, with Venice as the modern heir to ancient Rome's virtue.[147]

Both prior to the publication of *The Merchant of Venice* and in the decades after Shakespeare's death, a variety of writers asserted that Venice had a special affinity with ancient Rome and shared certain common characteristics with it. "As early as 1077, Pope Gregory VII attributed the liberty of the Venetians to their supposed roots in the ancient Roman nobility," according to Professor David McPherson:

> Many sixteenth- and seventeenth century writers ... claimed that the soul of ancient Rome had transmigrated into Venice. The germ of the idea is in a Latin poem by Julius Caesar Scalinger, one of Jonson's favorite Renaissance critics. Scalinger evokes the horror of the Barbarian invasions of Rome, but asserts that the Roman genius nevertheless was reborn in the midst of the sea (that is, in Venice). Several later writers pick up Scalinger's idea and develop it.[148]

The presumed affinity between these two cities in two different ages, noted by Julius Caesar Scalinger (1484-1558) before Shakespeare's birth, was repeated by several authors in the decades immediately after Shakespeare had written *The Merchant of Venice*. According to W. Chute's translation of Thomas de Fougasses' book, *The Generall Historie of the Magnificent State of Venice*, published in 1615:

> ... the Genius of it [ancient Rome] made transmigration to Venice. In her Wisedom, Fortitude, Justice, and Magnanimitie of old Rome

does yet move and stirre. That which now Usurps that name is not Rome, but her Carkasse, or rather Sepulcher. All but her Ruines, and the Cause of them, (her Vice) is removed to Venice.[149]

William Lithgow wrote in 1625 that "… the Romane Genius made a Pithagoricall transmigration into Venice."[150] John Raymond makes a similar assertion in his account of his travels in Italy, *An Itinerary Containing a Voyage Made through Italy in the Year 1646 and 1647*, published in London in 1648:

> The very mirrour of State and Policy, as she was borne about the death of old *Rome*; so shee seemes to bee hereditarily Possessour of that which maintained Rome in her soveraigne glory; The magnificent Genius of the People, the Gravity of the Senate, the solidity of her lawes, very much consonant with those of *Rome*.[151]

In the same spirit, James Howell compared and contrasted the features of ancient Roman and Venetian government in his book about Venice, published in 1651.[152] That Venice was the reincarnation of ancient Rome's spirit is evidently a fairly commonplace notion that persisted over time. It is not only possible, but plausible that Shakespeare could have made artistic use of this concept.

One reason why the city of Venice was commonly linked to ancient Rome lies in the historical circumstance of the city's origin: Venice was founded as a defensive response to the barbarian hordes that were invading Italy, just as the Roman Empire was collapsing. Machiavelli asserted that the city of Venice:

> owed its origin to the fact that several tribes had taken refuge on the little islands situated at the head of the Adriatic Sea, to escape from war, and from the Barbarians who after the fall of the Roman Empire had overrun Italy.[153]

Writing long after Machiavelli in a book published in 1648, Raymond elaborated upon the "coincidence of chronology" of the fall of the Roman empire and the founding of the city of

Venice.[154] That the birth of Venice was congruent with the demise of the Roman empire was a well-established bit of conventional wisdom.

Venice was the last vestige of civilization after the collapse and disintegration of Rome's empire. From an historical perspective, it began where ancient Rome left off. It was the latest, faintest remnant of the ancient Roman honor that had shined its brightest hundreds of years previously, gradually losing its luster. Venice was literally an island of civilization in a figurative sea of barbarians. As such, the city itself is a metaphor for the man of ancient Roman honor in the modern world. The concept of ancient Roman honor assumes that the individual stands alone as a personification of nobility typical of Rome's earliest heroes, isolated among the great mass of contemporary men who never equal this ancient standard. In a similar manner, Venice stands alone among the other contemporary cities. But even if, according to the traditional conception of Renaissance Venice, the city was considered to be the spiritual reincarnation of ancient Rome, Shakespeare is primarily concerned with the noble individual, rather than the noble city. Even though Venice may be the heir to ancient Rome (in Shakespeare's treatment), the majority of people in Venice fall short of this ideal, just as did most people in ancient Rome.

Like ancient Rome, Venice had a reputation for harsh justice that was is analogous to the "eye-for-an-eye" strain of Old Testament moral law. The city was famous in Shakespeare's day for impartial justice that treated all parties fairly without regard to their citizenship or social status,[155] but it was also known for its "severity. Swearing was sometimes punished in laymen by the loss of a hand, tongue, or eye."[156] Venetian justice, as a reflection of the Roman justice of an earlier era, is an appropriate premise upon which to base Shylock's legal claim to a pound of flesh. The Christian Venetians in the play may prefer that Antonio not give up a pound of his own flesh, but evidently they don't consider it particularly unusual for a legal ruling to cost someone a body part, as Antonio himself evidently did not when he first entered into his agreement with Shylock.

While Venice was perceived as the heir to the tradition of Roman nobility, it was no less the heir to the Roman tradition of festive indulgence. Like ancient Rome, which had its festival days as an alternative to harsh normative justice, Venice was also famous for its carnival, which featured comedies.[157] During the carnival, the Venetians wore masks and costumes, as Jessica, Lorenzo and other characters do on the night when Jessica flees Shylock's house.

Venice was known as a place both of great wealth and of gross immorality.[158] Its unique reputation as a center for both wealth and hedonistic pleasure lent to the city a mystique that fascinated Englishmen in Shakespeare's day:

> One could love it [Venice] as the locus of excitement and progressive culture, a sort of New York, London, and Paris combined, or hate it as the seat of excess and decadence, a Catholic Sodom and Gomorrah. Most English undoubtedly saw it as a bit of each. Shakespeare's view presents some of the evils and temptations of the place, but also exploits Venice's fascinating appeal.[159]

One writer of Shakespeare's era said of Venice that "no place of all Europe [is] able at this day to compare with that city for number of sumptuous houses, specially for their fronts."[160] By reputation, Venice was, in the words of John Day's 1608 comedy *Humor Out of Breath*, 'the best flesh-shambles in Italy,' with prostitution a highly visible and prominent aspect of the social scene.[161]

The highly visible presence in Venice of two elements—money and sexual pleasure—complement the two primary concerns of a Plautine comic hero—namely, debt and desire. It also reflects the twofold nature of Bassanio's personal situation, that of being in debt and in love. Venice's reputation as a city of money and sexual pleasure is also a reflection of the convergence of money and love in the ambiguous words and metaphors that Bassanio and Portia use when they speak of their love as a kind of wealth.[162]

Finally, the relationship between ancient Rome and Venice represents a convergence of extreme opposites—like late night and early morning, bright moonlight or pale daylight—that can be either identical or antithetical, depending upon one's perspective. Early Rome and early Venice were identical in that they were both isolated pockets of civilization that were founded in a world dominated by barbarians. However, the two cities are antithetical in the sense that they were founded at opposite ends of the Roman Empire's life cycle: the beginning of Venice represents the end of Rome. As such, the relationship between Rome and Venice is a metaphor for the self-contradictory ambiguity that is fundamental to the meaning of *The Merchant of Venice.* It is another example of how extreme opposites can converge on a single point of constant/variable identity, subject to the fluctuations of alternating paradigms and inverse irony.

Antony and irony

The historical Marc Antony, as Plutarch describes him, shared a trait with Shakespeare's Bassanio: he was a smooth talker who could disguise ignoble behavior behind a façade of fancy words. Also like Bassanio, Antony uses his facility with words to define on his own terms where the nobility of ancient Rome "appeared most." Plutarch says of Antony:

> He that could finely cloak his shameful deeds with fine words, said that the greatness and magnificence of the empire of Rome appeared most, not where the Romans took, but where they gave much: and nobility was multiplied amongst men, by the posterity of kings, when they left of their seed in divers places: and that by this means his first ancestor was begotten of Hercules, who had not left

the hope and continuance of his line and posterity, in the womb of
one only woman, fearing Solon's laws [against adultery], or regard-
ing the ordinances of men touching the procreation of children: but
that he gave it unto nature, and established the foundation of many
noble races and families in divers places.[163]

Here, in Plutarch's account, Antony reiterates the legend
about his own descent from Hercules. But Antony's purpose in
invoking his noble ancestry was to justify the claim that his
own adulterous sexual activity—his affair with Cleopatra—
exemplified the noble qualities associated with "the greatness
and magnificence of the empire of Rome." Of course, Antony
stretches the truth quite a bit in attempting to establish an
equivalence between siring illegitimate children and "the
greatness and magnificence of the empire of Rome." Antony's
self-serving claim runs against the grain of a fundamental assumption of ancient Roman honor: constant commitment to
one's word and bond, including promises of fidelity to the
marriage bond, an assumption that Brutus' Portia made pal-
pable when she cut a gash into her own thigh as proof of the
depth of her commitment to her personal ethos of ancient Roman honor (*JC*, II.i.279-286). One could say that Antony's concept of ancient Roman honor was antithetical to the ideal that
Portia exemplified—and therefore that Antony's concept of ancient Roman honor is least like Roman honor as the concept
was generally understood. Plutarch makes his own opinion of
Antony's self-justification quite clear when he introduces this
anecdote as an example of Antony's propensity to "cloak his
shameful deeds with fine words."

In his biographical chapter on Antony, Plutarch immediately
makes two points very clear: Antony looked like a noble hero—
and made a calculated effort to cultivate this appearance. But
contrary to appearances, Antony's lifestyle was dissipated and
dissolute, if not outright dishonorable. Plutarch says Antony:

had a noble presence, and showed a countenance of one of a noble house: he had a goodly thick beard, a broad forehead, crooke nosed, and there appeared such a manly look in his countenance, as is commonly seen in Hercules' pictures, stamped or graven in metal. Now it had been a speech of old time, that the family of the Antonii were descended from one Anton, the son of Hercules, whereof the family took name. This opinion did Antonius seek to confirm in all his doings: not only resembling him in the likeness of his body, as we have said before, but also in the wearing of his garments. For when he would openly show himself abroad before many people, he would always wear his cassock girt down low upon his hips, with a great sword hanging by his side, and upon that, some ill-favored cloak.[164]

Antony, then, took special care to project an image of nobility, taking as his model his fabled ancestor, the heroic Hercules. But Plutarch leaves little doubt that contrary to appearances, Antony's lifestyle was far from noble:

the noblemen (as Cicero saith) did not only mislike him, but also hate him for his naughty life: for they did abhor his bankets and drunken feasts he made at unseasonable times, and his extreme wasteful expenses upon vain light huswives, and then in the daytime he would sleep or walk out his drunkeness, thinking to wear away the fume of the abundance of wine which he had taken over night. In his house they did nothing but feast, dance, and mask: and himself passed away the time in hearing of foolish plays, or in marrying these players, tumblers, jesters, and such sort of people. As for proof hereof it is reported, that at Hippias' marriage, one of his jesters, he drank wine so lustily all night, that the next morning when he came to plead before the people assembled in council, who had sent for him: he being queasy-stomached with his surfeit he had taken, was compelled to lay all before them, and one of his friends held him his gown instead of a basin.[165]

Antony's "naughty life"—festive behavior at "unseasonable times"—compared poorly with the sobriety and restraint of the ancient Roman honor, which was personified by Pompey the Great, for example. Because Antony lived in Pompey's house (which he bought but declined to pay for), it was inevitable that Antony's character was compared unfavorably to Pompey's:

But setting aside the ill name he had for his insolency, he was yet much more hated in respect of the house he dwelt in, the which was the house of Pompey the Great: a man as famous for his temperance, modesty, and civil life, as for his three triumphs. For it grieved them to see the gates commonly shut against the captains, magistrates of the city, and also ambassadors of strange nations, which were sometimes thrust from the gate with violence: and that the house within was full of tumblers, antic dancers, jugglers, players, jesters, and drunkards, quaffing and guzzling, and that on them he spent and bestowed the most part of his money he got by all kind of possible extortions, bribery and policy.[166]

At a symbolic level, Antony lived in the house of ancient Roman honor. But his stature as the master of that house was considerably less than equal to the standard set by that house's original owner.

Shakespeare's characterization of Marc Antony is based on Plutarch's unflattering portrait. In *Antony and Cleopatra*, Caesar Augustus does not merely deride Antony as one who "wastes/ The lamps of night in revel" (I.iv.4-5). He goes so far as to say that Antony is a "a man who is the abstract of all faults" (I.iv.9). When Lepidus responds that Antony's shortcomings are relatively small compared to his virtues, Caesar Augustus says:

> You are too indulgent. Let's grant it is not
> Amiss to tumble on the bed of Ptolemy;
> To give a kingdom for a mirth; to sit
> And keep the turn of tippling with a slave;
> To reel the streets at noon, and stand the buffet
> With knaves that smell of sweat; say this becomes him,—
> As his composure must be rare indeed
> Whom these things cannot blemish,—yet must Antony
> No way excuse his foils, when we do bear
> So great weight in his lightness.   (*Ant.*, I.iv.16-25)

In a similar vein, Pompey shares Caesar's disdain for Antony's character, hoping that Antony's "libertine" ways will dissipate his energy and distract him from effectively pursuing his military goals:

> Tie up the libertine in a field of feasts,
> Keep his brain fuming; Epicurean cooks
> Sharpen with cloyless sauce his appetite,
> That sleep and feeding may prorogue his honour
> Even till a Lethe'd dullness! (*Ant.*, II.i.23-27)

In sum, Antony's libertine lifestyle serves to "prorogue his honor," according to Pompey—that is, to put his honor on hold.

In effect, Antony's behavior has far more in common with the excesses typical of characters in Roman comedy than with the self-restraint stipulated by Roman honor. His "naughty life" of "unseasonable" feasts and masks, drunken companionship with clowns and comic actors is analogous to the "naughty times / [that] Put bars between the owners and their rights" (*MV*, 3.2.18-9): that is, the festive inversion of values typical of a Roman holiday.

Like numerous characters in Roman comedy, Antony accumulated heavy debts from his lifestyle of frivolous excess. More to the point, like Bassanio in *The Merchant of Venice*, Antony lived beyond his means to the point where a friend had to guarantee his debts. Plutarch explains the circumstances of this situation:

> Now Antonius being a fair young man, and in the prime of his youth: he fell acquainted with Curio, whose friendship and acquaintance (as it is reported) was a plague unto him. For he was a dissolute man, given over to all lust and insolency, who to have Antonius the better at his commandment, trained him on into great follies, and vain expenses upon women, in rioting and banketing. So that in short time, he brought Antonius into a marvellous great debt, and too great for one of his years, to wit: of two hundred and fifty talents, for all which sum Curio was his surety.[167]

Curio played the role in history that Antonio plays in *The Merchant of Venice*; he is the person with the means to guarantee the credit of a friend who did not manage his own money prudently. Curio was to Antony in ancient Rome what Antonio was to Bassanio in Shakespearean comedy: he takes financial responsibility for the debts incurred by his friend, an irresponsible spendthrift. The historical Antony and the comic Antonio are therefore mirror images of one another. They are complementary antipodes who face each other from opposite sides of the debtor/debt-guarantor relationship. In other words, Curio was Antony's "Antonio" and Antonio was Bassanio's "Curio."

Antonio in *The Merchant of Venice* is said to be the one in whom the ancient Roman honor most appears. But among noble Romans, his namesake, Marc Antony could be called the one in whom the ancient Roman honor *least* appeared, living a life of drunkenness, self-indulgence, and general dissipation, according to Plutarch's account. If ancient Roman honor is the *ne plus ultra* of normative self-restraint and the sharpest possible antithesis to festive self-indulgence, then Marc Antony is the sharpest possible antithesis to the standard that Roman comedy was supposed to invert.

Whereas traditional Roman comedy celebrates the inverse of normative ideals, *The Merchant of Venice* gives play to a double inversion. The pattern expected for Roman comedy would have inverted the world of a sober, stalwart of ancient Roman honor. In taking Marc Antony as a literary analogue to Antonio, Shakespeare inverts a model that is already an inversion, just as he did in making a Jewish money lender the play's foremost exemplar of ancient Roman honor. Antonio is the one in whom the ancient Roman honor is said to most appear—but his personal bearing is antithetical to ancient Roman honor. Shylock, on the other hand, is the one who actually most represents ancient Roman honor, but his persona is antithetical to any appearance of Roman nobility. The Jewish money lender—like the drunken, adulterous Antony—is an inversion of the conventional image of ancient Roman honor, even though he serves the dramatic function of representing that ideal.

Part five

"Meaning" in *The Merchant of Venice*

The Merchant of Venice is a moral and epistemological Mobius strip. It is self-contradictory, but consistent—melding appearance and reality together in an ambiguous unity of opposites that is simultaneously true and false, grossly obvious and subtly deceptive.[168] The ultimate irony is that Shakespeare deceives his audience with a play that plainly says that people are easily deceived. What could be more simple and obvious— yet simultaneously more obscure and complex? The play as a whole, like Bassanio's speech on outward appearance, manages to lie while telling the truth, turning the truth inside out as well as upside down. Bassanio speaks for himself as well as for the play as a whole when he states: "The world is still deceived with ornament" (3.2.74). "Ornament," he says:

> is but the guiled shore
> To a most dangerous sea, the beauteous scarf
> Veiling an Indian beauty; in a word,
> The seeming truth which cunning times put on
> To entrap the wisest.   (3.2.97-101)

The meaning of *The Merchant of Venice* lies in the function of its genre, comic drama: to invert normative morality with festive irony. In the final analysis, the meaning of the play is not reductive to issues external to the art of drama, issues such as ancient Roman honor, Christian mercy, or Jewish legalism. The play's meaning is ultimately self-reductive: its meaning is exactly what the play itself says is meaningful—that outward appearance is least itself, and that the world is deceived with ornament. The play's meaning is self-evident: it is "about" exactly those themes that it says it is "about." Yet the play clearly states that what seems to be self-evident could be misleading.

And as it turns out, the meaning of the play is actually quite far from self-evident—just as the play had stated plainly several times.

The honor/irony interpretation of *The Merchant of Venice* is based on the assumption that Shakespeare is in complete command of his art and is fully capable of leading—or misleading—an audience in any direction that serves his artistic purpose. His incomparable mastery of language enables him to create a superficial illusion that glitters and shimmers like gold, as it were—powerful enough to mesmerize and bamboozle. Shakespeare conjures a spell that has a tendency to distract audiences and readers from his intended dramatic purpose— a literary legerdemain that might itself be his intended dramatic purpose.

Shakespeare creates the impression that certain issues are obvious and self-evident, when actually these issues are the "ornament" that hides a subtle and somewhat obscure reality, which is contrary to appearance. Therefore audiences are deceived by Bassanio's professions of sincerity. Likewise, people take at face value Portia's poetic speech on the quality of mercy—even though we supposedly know better than to be deceived by outward show. The audience is led to believe that the play is "about" the clash between Christian and Jew; and the author arouses the audience's feelings of righteous indignation and moral superiority. That an audience strongly, vehemently and with utmost certainty believes an opinion to be true (of course) does not validate the truth of that opinion. On the contrary, in the case of *The Merchant of Venice*, the audience's presumed moral superiority confirms and amplifies the play's message—that modern, Christian Europe is smug and superficial, morally obtuse and gullible.

Although comic irony is usually obvious to the audience while the characters in the play are oblivious to it, in *The Merchant of Venice* Shakespeare extends that irony such that the audience is as oblivious as the characters in the play. Shakespeare manipulates people in the audience as skillfully as if they were characters on the stage—as if human behavior could be scripted no less predictably than the actions of characters in a play, as if all the world were indeed a stage.

The honor/irony interpretation finds in *The Merchant of Venice* a sensibility similar to that which Professor Stephen Booth finds in *Julius Caesar*: that of a cryptic author, alienated from his audience, testing the limits of his power to deceive the crowd. Shakespeare can manipulate his audience "as easily as Antony manipulates the plebeians," according to Booth's interpretation of *Julius Caesar*.[169] Booth contends that "'we—an audience contemptuous of the forgetfulness and inconsistency in the characters put before us by the play—are as indifferent to intellectual constancy as the contemptible, audience-like mob.'"[170]

> "*Julius Caesar* seems to me [Booth says] to be its author's cynical experiment with the limits of his power to make puppets of theater audiences." Booth strongly suspects that "Shakespeare felt malicious pleasure in making us victims of a practical joke so mean that it denies its victims the ultimate dignity of knowing they have been victimized and thus knowing that their attacker considers them worth dignifying." Shakespeare constructs a play that "would make its audiences make fools of themselves and compound their folly by blindness to it."[171]

The bottom line is that "while we are feeling contempt for the characters, the author is feeling contempt for us," Booth says of *Julius Caesar*.[172]

Analogous to what Booth observes in regard to *Julius Caesar*, audiences of *The Merchant of Venice* also give vent to feelings of moral indignation—either condemning the Jew for his cruelty or condemning the Christians for their hypocrisy. They remain oblivious to the possibility that their feelings (which are without doubt sincere and strongly felt) might be entirely misguided. The net effect is another inversion of extreme opposites, with one extreme mistaken for the other: audiences do not consider that their presumed moral superiority to Shylock or Portia (as the case may be) is proof and confirmation of their own moral inferiority; they don't consider that the vehemence of their response to the play is a validation of Shakespeare's ability to manipulate and deceive them rather than a validation of the loftiness of their own moral judgment.

This artistic enterprise is an expression of contempt for an audience that allows itself to be manipulated so. It is a logical consequence of a play that extends to the sharpest possible extreme the implications of two related concepts: irony and honor—first, the fundamental deceptiveness of inverse irony, which is based on the ironies of mistaken identity and inversions of conventional wisdom inherent to ancient Roman comedy and the genre of comic drama; and second, the fundamental disdain for the common man inherent to the concept of ancient Roman honor, a retrogressive, elitist ideal that was the normative foil to Roman comedy's festive irony. The disdain of the artist for his audience is a common denominator to both the ideal of ancient Roman honor and the deceptiveness of inverse irony. The man of ancient Roman honor's contempt for his modern contemporaries is reflected in the portrait of the volatile crowd (in *Julius Caesar* and *Coriolanus*, for example). The crowd personifies those qualities that are contrary to honor, that which is false and variable; the crowd in the plays is a metaphor for the audience, and by extension, for all of mankind.

Even though Shakespeare repeatedly makes the point in *The Merchant of Venice* that appearance is misleading, in most respects the play has been accepted at face value—as if the play's fundamental message about the deceptiveness of superficial appearance were relevant everywhere except in regard to the play itself, which is somehow presumed to be exempt from its own message. This blindness to the obvious, at the root of Shakespeare's artistic intent for this play, is analogous to the

grossest sort of moral hypocrisy as well as to human consciousness itself. Hypocrisy is unsubtle and lacking in self-awareness, while self-conscious introspection is subtle and self-reflective; but both are incapable of objective self-observation.
"For the eye sees not itself," says Brutus, "But by reflection, by
some other things" (*JC*, I.ii.52-53). In this light, *The Merchant
of Venice* represents a convergence of two opposite extremes
of the human spirit that converge at a similar blind spot—acute
self-awareness and acute lack-of-self-awareness. The art form
of dramatic comedy, which holds a mirror to life, is therefore
is ultimately reductive to a reflection of human consciousness
itself, the faculty through which life is perceived.

The great chain of illusion

The honor/irony paradigm leads to an interpretation of *The
Merchant of Venice* that stands upon a pyramid of reciprocal
abstractions. This chain of analogies, inversions and ironies
reflects a pattern of thought that was typical of Shakespeare's
time, when it was not unusual to perceive the world in terms
of analogies and inverse analogies; correspondences and dis-
junctions; hierarchies and inversions of hierarchies. Analogical thinking—looking at the world in terms of analogies—was
"for Shakespeare and his audience, a prevailing intellectual
mode."[173] Despite the on-going dissolution of the medieval
world view that originally shaped the analogical mind-set, Professor Elton says:

> the analogical habit of mind, with its correspondences, hierarchies,
> and microcosmic-macrocosmic relationships survived. Levels of ex-
> istence, including human and cosmic, were habitually correlated,
> and correspondences and resemblances were perceived everywhere.
> Man as microcosmic model was thus a mediator between himself
> and the universe; and knowledge of one element in the microcosm-
> macrocosm analogy was knowledge of the other. Blending faith with
> knowledge, actuality with metaphysics, analogy also joined symbol

and concept, the internal with the external world. Analogy, indeed, provided the perceiver with the impression of aesthetically and philosophically comprehending experience.[174]

Analogical thinking in the Renaissance, based on the premises of a medieval worldview, gave structure to ideas that contradicted that worldview.[175] Analogies and correspondences that once gave order and meaning to the universe were used to describe a world in which relativism and disorder challenged values that formerly seemed absolute and immutable. "In numerous spheres of Elizabethan thought occurred transitions and revaluations, if not actual crises and reversals," according to Professor Elton.[176] Modern and medieval ideas clashed and co-mingled during the Renaissance, which brought together "contradictory and disparate Christian and non-Christian currents."[177]

Shakespeare's drama reflected the "intellectual tensions of his analogical yet transitional age."[178] It "provided an appropriate conflict structure" that enabled Shakespeare to capture and illuminate the intellectual and spiritual themes of his day in "a dialectic of ironies and ambivalences:

> avoiding in its complex movement and multi-voiced dialogue the simplifications of direct statement and reductive resolution .... Renaissance epistemological crisis might be evoked through the emphasis on illusion and appearance-versus-reality of the theatrical setting itself, as well as through ambiguous juxtaposition of scenes, particularly in multiple plot structure. Embracing and juxtaposing the contradictions of his age, Shakespeare contrived an artistic virtue out of a contemporary necessity. Within his heterogeneous audience, playing off one antithetical preconception against another, he structured his works partly only on numerous current issues of controversy. Manipulating such diverse attitudes, while engaging the attention of all, he achieved an integrated, yet complex and multifaceted dramatic form.[179]

The honor/irony interpretation of *The Merchant of Venice* reflects this pattern of Renaissance thought, linking together several levels of meaning in an hierarchical chain of microcosm and macrocosm, and finding meaning in analogical and inverse-analogical relationships—Venice/Rome, Antonio/Marc Antony, Jews/Romans, Shylock/Antonio, etc.

Bassanio personifies in microcosm the ambiguous, self-contradictory meaning of *The Merchant of Venice*: he states plainly that superficial appearances are false, appearing to be sincere even though he himself is not what he appears to be. He claims to care little for money, but desperately needs Portia's financial assistance. He professes to be unimpressed by external appearance, although he has consistently tried to manipulate appearance for his own advantage.

The play as a whole reflects Bassanio's self-contradictory ambivalence at a macrocosmic level: it is a play about the deceptiveness of superficial appearance that is itself deceptive in appearance. It appears to be a play about the conflict between Christian ideal and Jewish stereotype, although below the surface it explores the issues of ancient Roman honor and festive Roman license and immorality. The play appears to be simple and straightforward, even while repeatedly making the point that perception of reality is a complex challenge; it states clearly that what appears to be clear may be an illusion.

At the next level up on the chain of analogy, the play exemplifies in microcosm the genre of dramatic comedy, which is based on festive irony, mistaken identity and comic reversal of conventional wisdom. The genre inverts the normative relationship between harsh reality and wishful thinking, creating a context that excuses the inexcusable and praises the deplorable. Shakespeare extends this logic to a self-contradictory point of absurdity in *The Merchant of Venice*, inverting the inverse of Roman comedy's customary inversions.

The genre of dramatic comedy, in turn, exemplifies in microcosm the ambiguous nature of life itself and the self-contradictions of human perception, including both the grossest sort of moral hypocrisy as well as the subtlest type of introspective self-consciousness, both of which are incapable of objective self-observation. As Professor Elton (cited above) has said, Shakespeare identified a correspondence between the conventions of the genre and the contradictory and conflicting intellectual and moral issues of his day; the genre provided Shakespeare with "an appropriate conflict structure" that enabled him to portray these issues as they were, "without the simplifications of direct statement and reductive resolution."[180]

Writing on Shakespeare's mature comedy, Kermode takes note of

> Shakespeare's pre-occupation with the comedy of mistaken identity, first as a brilliant apprentice-imitator in *Comedy of Errors*, later with an increasingly deep brooding over the truth hidden in the dramatic convention: for if it is accepted that all of our dealings with reality are affected by an inability certainly to distinguish between what is said and what is meant, between things as they are and as they appear to be, between Truth and Opinion, then the comic errors develop a peculiar relevance to life itself.[181]

The Merchant of Venice is fully consistent with the "increasingly deep brooding of the dramatic convention" that Kermode identifies as a pattern of Shakespeare's comedy. It is ironic that Kermode sees *The Merchant* as an exception to this general pattern of skepticism about perception in so far as he asserts that the meaning of the play is "obvious" and moreover, that it is about themes that are obvious; and therefore is different from the other Shakespeare plays of this period, which are examples of "deep brooding" about the variance between what seems to be and what is. Kermode says that it is "only by a determined effort to avoid the obvious [that] we can mistake the theme of *The Merchant of Venice*," which in his view is the triumph of love and mercy over "usury and corrupt love."[182] However, in terms of the honor/irony paradigm, Shakespeare's intention is precisely to make "a determined effort to avoid the obvious" in order to fully realize his artistic objective—to portray the illusory nature of life, where that which superficially seems to be obviously true is actually false.

From this perspective, a chain of analogies extends from the self-contradictory nature of Bassanio's speech (which is both obvious and misleading) to Bassanio himself, the play in its entirety, the genre of comic drama and ultimately to human consciousness and life itself. To bring this chain of analogies full circle: just as drama is life in microcosm, life—in turn—is drama in macrocosm, a reflection of drama and its conventions of genre. As Antonio says at the beginning of *The Merchant of Venice*: "I hold the world but as the world Graziano, / A stage, where every man must play a part, / And mine a sad one" (I.i.77-79). Jaques elaborates on this perspective in *As You Like It*, in a speech that begins:

> All the world's a stage,
> And all the men and women merely players.
> They have their exits and their entrances,
> And one man in his time plays many parts ...   (*AYL*, II.vii.139-142)

The metaphor of the world as a stage extends dramatic irony to its most extreme conclusion. It is a logical consequence of the deep irony that Shakespeare explores at every level in *The Merchant of Venice*, a reflection of a dramatic irony that is radically skeptical about conventionally-presumed distinctions between opposite extremes: black and white, moonlight and sunlight, obvious and obscure, illusion and truth, wakefulness and dreaming, art and life. The breakdown of these fundamental distinctions between ostensibly opposite extremes makes all things possible, including the inversion and confusion of extreme opposites: carnality and spirituality; money and love; Christian morality and pagan immorality; Jewish respect for human dignity and Roman respect for property rights; comedy and tragedy; humor and despair; ancient festivals and modern solipsism.

In sum, the fundamental issue of deceptive appearance is linked through a chain of analogies that extends from

Bassanio's personal deceptiveness to the deceptiveness of the play as a whole, the irony typical to the genre, and the illusory nature of reality. This chain of analogies, extending from the smallest microcosm to the vastest macrocosm, is analogous to the Great Chain of Being, the theological/analogical perspective that shaped medieval thought. However, while religious faith is the fundamental premise that gives order and meaning to the Great Chain of Being, the comic vision of *The Merchant of Venice* begins with deception and ends with illusion. It is based on bad faith—falsehood masquerading as truth. The comic vision of *The Merchant of Venice* is therefore antithetical to the medieval world view, and a comic inversion of the Great Chain of Being.

The Merchant of Venice is commonly believed to be an example of Christian apologetics (at best) or of Christian anti-Semitism (at worst). But it is difficult to understand how an epistemological structure based on deceptiveness and illusion could be construed as a justification for Christian belief of any kind. If outward appearance is least itself, then words (the outward appearance, as it were, of religious belief) can be misleading. Consequently, truth—even religious truth—is not absolute because it is mediated by words and relative to human perception and individual perspective—and therefore inherently illusory and unstable. Furthermore, if words can be ambiguous to the extent that there is no apparent difference between sexual arousal and "an upright life" of religious devotion, then anything goes: an orderly, Christian universe must necessarily dissolve into agnostic chaos.

The Great Chain of Being and a great chain of illusion are irreconcilable antitheses. Radical skepticism about man's ability to perceive reality is antithetical to the certainty of religious faith, because even faith (whether based upon reason or pure faith) is based upon human perception. In *The Merchant of Venice* Shakespeare relentlessly drives concepts to the furthest extent of their logic; it is reasonable to presume that he was therefore astute enough to understand that when radical skepticism begins to erode faith in main's ability to perceive truly then religious belief begins to crumble, and with it, ethics, morality and epistemology based on religious belief. In effect, *The Merchant of Venice* is much more an attack on the fundamental premises of Christian faith than it is an example of Christian apologetics or anti-Semitism.

Conclusions

The Merchant of Venice demonstrates Shakespeare's awesome mastery of comic theory and practice. Canonical writers, according to Bloom, are both nurtured and challenged by the masterworks of literary tradition before they break with past precedent in a way that establishes their own originality. "Tradition is not only a handing-down or process of benign transmission," according to Bloom. "It is also a conflict between past genius and present aspiration, in which the prize is literary survival or canonical inclusion."[183] In *The Merchant of Venice*, Shakespeare (who is thoroughly grounded in Plutarch and Plautus, pillars of the Canon of his time) begins with the model of Roman comedy. However, he extends the logic of Roman comedy's festive irony to a point where it transforms and transcends the bounds of the genre as it had existed previously, taking comedy from a crudely obvious social parody to a subtly deceptive literary *tour de force* of multi-dimensional irony, unequaled before or since.

The Merchant of Venice is masterwork of technical virtuosity, rhetorical skill and artistic vision that exploits the full potential of its art form, stretching the limitations of its genre to the breaking point and beyond. It is brilliantly executed: meticulously plotted, rigorously structured and thematically integrated. And it achieves a coldly calculated effect. This con-

ception of Shakespeare's artistic achievement supports that of
Professor Harry Levin, who has written that:

> During the last hundred years we have been learning to examine
> Shakespeare more and more closely. On the whole he has withstood
> that scrutiny, and rewarded it with a renewed awareness of his in-
> sight and technique. Today we think of him as a highly conscious
> artist .... We are likely to understand him better if we assume that he
> knew what he was doing every minute, even at the risk of an occa-
> sional exercise in overingenuity on our part.[184]

"Overingenuity," however, is not in itself an absolute valua-
tion. It is relative to the perception that an interpretation is
either persuasive or not. It is also relative to readers' comfort
level with the degree of variation from their accustomed manner of thinking about such things.

The Christian/Jewish interpretive paradigm, which has
shaped criticism of *The Merchant of Venice* so far, fails to resolve significant thematic contradictions and inconsistencies:
it cannot reconcile Shylock's cruelty with his humanity; it cannot reconcile the Christians' ideals with their behavior; it cannot thematically integrate the Christian/Jewish themes of hate
versus love with Bassanio's casual wish to see Portia dead and
his broken promise never to part with her ring. The problem
with interpretations based on the Christian/Jewish interpretive paradigm is that in failing to resolve these questions they
have been too easily satisfied with a fairly superficial examination of the play and too quick to come to conclusions based
on material external to the play.

The honor/irony approach to the play contradicts what was
at one time a fairly common assumption about Shakespeare's
artistry, that "in a word, the method of Shakespeare's drama
consists, essentially, in the humanization of melodrama."[185] According to this point of view, Shakespeare is believed to re-
cycle plots taken from history and legend, and then is said to
"breath life" into these tales with his superior poetry and depth

of characterization.[186] The structure of Shakespeare's plays, like the content of his plot material, was supposed to have been derived from pre-existing sources. Therefore, Shakespeare's "added value" was presumed to lie in beauty of poetry and "life-like" characterization. On the basis of these premises, it would be logical to conclude, with Middleton Murry, that:

> The unity of a Shakespeare play (if we may generalize) is seldom what would be described today as a unity of conception. That was precluded, save in rare cases, by the necessities of Shakespeare's peculiar craft.[187]

No doubt the critic's work is vastly simplified if a play is not presumed to be an integrated and unified work of art, a presumption that precludes the effort that would otherwise be necessary to delineate that artistic unity and integrity. This point of view vastly underestimates the depth of Shakespeare's artistry, even as critics who hold these assumptions praise Shakespeare's achievement to the skies. For example, Professor Goddard finds a great deal of meaning in Shakespeare, but finds it necessary to state that Shakespeare is primarily a poet and only incidentally a dramatist, remarking:

> that Shakespeare is primarily a poet ought to be so obvious that even to put the thought in words would be banal....the critics whose central interest is dramaturgy...have obscured the greater Shakespeare.[188]

Just as Goddard postulates a schizoid distinction between Shakespeare the poet and Shakespeare the dramatist, Professor Charlton seeks to explain the ostensible contradictions in Shylock's character by postulating two Shakespeares, one a professional dramatist working within the limitations of his time and place in Elizabethan England; the other, a universal artist whose imagination transcends the limits of provincial prejudice. The former supposedly intended Shylock to be a crowd-pleasing anti-Semitic stereotype, while the latter sup-

posedly followed the commands of a higher vision, endowing
Shylock with a dignity and humanity that contradicts the stereotype.[189] The problem with this rationale for the ostensibly
contradictory aspects of Shylock's personality is that it seeks
to resolve questions about the interpretation of the play on the
basis of unfounded speculation about the artist's creative process, citing a presumed duality in the artist's personality—
Shakespeare the poet versus Shakespeare the dramatist,
Shakespeare the provincial Englishman versus Shakespeare
the universal genius—to explain and justify contradictions that
an interpretation of the play fails to reconcile.

Although this approach to interpretation would be considered archaic today, it continues to influence *Merchant of Venice*
criticism because it is a solution of last resort, a fall-back position that explains contradictions that cannot be explained otherwise within the context of the Christian/Jewish paradigm.
"Shakespeare possibly intended to give us a pathetic monster
in Shylock," says Professor Bloom, one of the most sophisticated and insightful critics writing today:

> but being Shakespeare, he gave us Shylock concerned whom little
> can be said that will not be at least oxymoronic, if not indeed self-
> contradictory. That Shylock got away from Shakespeare seems clear
> enough, but that is the scandal of Shakespearean representation; so
> strong is it that nearly all his creatures break out of the temporal
> trap of Elizabethan and Jacobean mimesis, and establish standards
> of imitation that do seem to be, not of an age, but for all time.[190]

Professor Bloom is, of course, right on target in noting the
oxymoronic and self-contradictory aspects of Shylock's characterization. However, his explanation "that Shylock got away
from Shakespeare" begs the question of what those contradictions might mean. The honor/irony perspective presumes that
The Merchant of Venice is a highly-integrated work of art. According to this point of view, Shylock didn't "get away" from
Shakespeare because nothing in this play got away from

Shakespeare; every word and phrase is nailed down securely in a structure that has been designed to achieve a consciously defined artistic and dramatic purpose.

Interpreting the contradictions in Shylock's personality is directly related to the question of anti-Semitism, which has been one of the most divisive questions for *Merchant of Venice* criticism, particularly in the 50 years following the Holocaust of World War II. Within the Christian/Jewish paradigm, questions of interpretation often boil down to Shylock, pro or con; victim or villain. The honor/irony paradigm moves the issue of the play's anti-Semitism from the foreground to the background, reinterpreting the play entirely in a framework that is not subject to Christian or Jewish terms. However, after an exhaustive analysis of the play, the honor/irony paradigm offers a relatively simple answer to the question of anti-Semitism in the play: the play is without doubt superficially anti-Semitic; its inner meaning is therefore without doubt antithetical to superficial appearance, and is consequently not anti-Semitic. The play's principle of inverse irony—that outward show is least itself—teaches that superficial appearance is contrary to a deeper reality. According to this logic, the play could appear to be anti-Semitic, even though it is anti-anti-Semitic in intent. In other words, the play is anti-Semitic on the surface, but its artistic intent is entirely focused on the notion that what is on the surface is false, and that people who believe what is on the surface are mistaken.

Shakespeare's sympathies lie with the non-Christian ideal of ancient Roman honor, which he identifies with Shylock, the Jew. And this ideal does not support the Christian majority's persecution of a religious or ethnic minority; instead, it is an anti-Christian, anti-majoritarian, retrogressive elitism. There can be no doubt that Shakespeare bases his characterization of Shylock on an anti-Semitic stereotype. Shakespeare knows how to push his audience's "hot buttons." And Shylock, the cruel money lender who demands justice and spurns mercy, is a character that pushes hot buttons today no less powerfully than he did 400 years ago. However, just as it is clear that Shakespeare does indeed engage in Jew baiting with this play, it is equally clear that he disdains the gullibility and malleability of the mob mentality that anti-Semitism thrives on. It is true that Shakespeare manipulates the crowd with anti-Semitic stereotype, but he does so out of contempt for the crowd, to mock people in irony for their superficiality and irrationality, as well as to demonstrate the ease with which crowds can be deceived and stupidly emotional about something that in fact is completely antithetical to what they imagine it to be.

Shakespeare's sensibility as reflected in this artistic enterprise—arousing and manipulating crowd emotion that he does not share, juxtaposing moral antitheses and obscuring the differences between them—is similar to the self-reflective ambivalence evident in Sonnet #94:

> They that have pow'r to hurt and will do none,
> That do not do the thing they most do show,
> Who, moving others, are themselves as stone,
> Unmoved, cold, and to temptation slow,
> They rightly do inherit heaven's graces
> And husband nature's riches from expense;
> They are the lords and owners of their faces,
> Others but stewards of their excellence.
> The summer's flow'r is to the summer sweet
> Though to itself it only live and die,
> But if that flow'r with base infection meet,
> The basest weed outbraves his dignity:
>   For sweetest things turn sourest by their deeds,
>   Lilies that fester smell far worse than weeds.

Appendix

Inverse irony in Shakespeare's other work

Shakespearean drama is very often concerned with the confusion of mistaken identity, the illusion of appearance and the
elusiveness of reality. These issues are a common denominator to Shakespeare's comedy and tragedy, in such plays as *The
Comedy of Errors* and *A Midsummer Night's Dream* no less
than in *Romeo and Juliet* and *Othello*. Danson's book on *The
Merchant of Venice* (which is a Christian interpretation of the
play) mentions *Richard III, Othello, The Winter's Tale* and *Much
Ado About Nothing* as examples that support this point:[191]

> The limits of sensory experience and the folly of trusting to even
> the most reasonable shows of the world are alluded to several times
> in the play. It is a part of the "moral" of the casket-trials. Those who
> "choose by show" (2.9.26), taking their evidence only from what can
> be seen or heard, will never choose aright. Those "worldly choos-
> ers" are contrasted with another sort who "choose not by the view"
> (3.2.131); the latter enact a secular demonstration of the faith which,
> according to St. Paul, "is the grounde of all things, which are hoped
> for, and the evidence of things which are not sene" (Heb. ii : 1).[192]

Shakespeare makes the point repeatedly, in numerous plays,
that outward appearance can diverge from reality. In this respect, *The Merchant of Venice* falls within the mainstream of
Shakespeare's thematic focus. However, in the context of the
honor/irony interpretation of the play, appearance and reality
aren't merely dissonant in *The Merchant of Venice*—they are
extreme opposites, antitheses. According to the principle of
inverse irony and its corollaries, that which superficially appears to be most true is actually most false; and that which
superficially most seems to be false is true; further, that extreme opposites can share a common outward appearance and
can be confused for one another; and that extreme opposites

can be inverted and still confused for one another.

It is beyond the scope of the present study to reinterpret a broad cross-section of Shakespeare plays in the light of this principle. But the principle of inverse irony is not unique to *The Merchant of Venice*. Other plays share *The Merchant*'s fairly specific focus on inverse irony and its various corollaries, sharing as well the metaphors of inverse irony: inversions and confusions between moonlight and sunlight, black and white, ravens and doves—holding day with the Antipodes, as Bassanio had put it.

It may be true, as John Gross says in his book on Shylock, "that wholesale irony, running right through a play, is not Shakespeare's practice anywhere else."[193] Nevertheless, at least several other Shakespeare plays are thoroughly imbued with the logic of inverse irony that is exploited to such an extreme degree in *The Merchant of Venice*. These other plays may not be as cryptic in their irony as *The Merchant of Venice*, but through metaphor, plot and character, they illustrate an artistic vision shared in common with *The Merchant of Venice*, which—though obviously different in execution from other plays—is not unique in its exploration of the principle of inverse irony.

A Midsummer Night's Dream (the play that directly precedes *The Merchant of Venice* in the First Folio) repeatedly makes the point that truth and appearance are not merely dissonant—they are extreme opposites. In act three, the centerpiece of the play, Bottom, the buffoonish working class windbag with the head of a jackass, is braying harshly—a fairly extreme antithesis to anyone's ideal of a romantic love interest. But Titania, the fairy queen, perceives Bottom's harsh heehawing as beautiful music:

> I pray thee gentle mortal, sing again;
> Mine ear is much enamour'd of thy note;
> So is mine eye enthralled to thy shape;

And thy fair virtue's force perforce doth move me
On the first view to say, to swear, I love thee.   (*MND*, III.1.140-144)

The disparity of extreme opposites—fairy queen and jackass, beatiful music and jackass' bray—accentuates the dissonance between Titania and the one she believes she loves. What Titania sees and hears could not be any more antithetical to the reality of the matter. She sees what her mind perceives; and she perceives ugliness as beauty, harshness as sweetness. For her, outward show is truly least itself. She judges by the "view"—a superficial perception that is completely wrong, but so utterly convincing that she does not merely say that she loves Bottom, she *swears* that she does. (When Bassanio correctly selects the unattractive casket of lead to win the beautiful Portia, the scroll inside begins: "You that choose not by the view" (*MV*, 3.2.131).)

The other lovers in *A Midsummer Night's Dream*—Helena and Hermia, Demetrius and Lysander—repeatedly play out the principle of inverse irony. Lysander flees into the woods with Hermia, who, according to stage tradition, is short and dark. He loves her more than the Athenian law will permit. But once in the woods, suddenly the opposite is true: Lysander abandons Hermia for Helena, who, according to stage tradition, is tall and fair. He then loves Helena, Hermia's antithesis, with the same intensity of passion that just a short while before he had directed to Hermia, who is amazed at this abrupt reversal of commitment.

The sun was not so true unto the day
As he to me: would he have stolen away
From sleeping Hermia? I'll believe as soon
This whole earth may be bor'd and that the moon
May through the centre creep and so displease
Her brother's noontide with the Antipodes.   (III.ii.50-55)

Hermia echoes Bassanio's statement that "We should hold day with the Antipodes, / If you would walk in absence of the sun"

(*MV*, 5.1.127-128). Hermia had believed that Lysander's devotion to her was as constant and reliable as sunrise every morning. She had believed that a change in his affections would be as unlikely an inversion as the sun and moon changing places: there isn't anything more certain than the morning sunrise, and there aren't opposites any more antithetical than the sun and the moon, day and night, white and black; yet despite Hermia's certainty that the sun is the sun and the moon is the moon, Lysander has in fact dumped her for Helena, notwithstanding his previous promises of fidelity. Metaphorically speaking, moonlight has displaced what Hermia believes to be sunshine (Lysander's love). Lysander had emphatically promised that he would remain faithful to Hermia—"end life when I end loyalty!" (II.ii.63)—echoing Bassanio's promise of devotion that: "when this ring / Parts from this finger, then parts life from hence" (*MV*, 3.2.183-184). Of course, shortly afterward (like Bassanio), Lysander violates his firm commitment: "I had no judgment when to her [Hermia] I swore," he says to Helena (III.ii.134).

At the beginning of the play in act one, both Lysander and Demetrius claim to love Hermia. Neither of them loves Helena. At the middle of the play in act three, both men claim with equal passion that they love Helena. Small and dark, once beautiful, is now rejected; tall and fair, once ignored, is now celebrated as beautiful. It is a startling reversal of affection, demonstrating that opposites—tall and fair, short and dark—are essentially equivalent and interchangeable.

But that's not how Lysander perceives the matter: his love for Hermia has suddenly inverted to its opposite—hate (III.ii.270). "Who will not change a raven for a dove?" Lysander says to Helena (II.ii.123), in a complete inversion of preference, white for black.[194] The men remain constant in their passion, even though their desire abruptly shifts from one woman to a second woman who (in outward appearance, at least) is

completely antithetical to the first woman. They are as inconstant in their loyalty as the crowd in *Julius Caesar*, which at
first passionately supports Brutus, only to shift its fervent loyalty shortly afterward to Antony, Brutus' enemy.

Meanwhile, Helena perceives Demetrius' declaration of love
for her as its opposite—mockery (III.ii.136-161). He tries hard
to show Helena how much he loves her, but despite his exer-
tions—perhaps because of them—she remains skeptical. For
her, outward show is least itself: she does not believe Demetrius
when he asserts that he cannot love her; neither does she believe him when he asserts that he loves her passionately. She
was unhappy when he did not love her; she is no happier when
his love for her exactly fulfills her previous wishes. Helena
remains constant in her feeling of rejection, even though
Demetrius has completely reversed his outward behavior to
her.

The inversion and confusion of extreme opposites in *Midsummer Night's Dream*—dark and fair, tall and short, love and
hate, night and day—is analogous to the metaphor of "daylight sick" (*MV*, 5.1.124) that Portia uses to describe the inversion of perceptual paradigms. Perception is defined by paradigm, and shifting paradigms can translate superficial appearances into their opposites, which can be inverted and confused.
Lysander inverts opposites when he asserts that the darkness
of the night is bright—because Helena "more engilds the night /
Than all yon fiery oes and eyes of light" (III.ii.187-188). His
comments complement what Helena had earlier said of
Demetrius: "It is not night when I do see your face / Therefore
I think I am not in the night—" (II.i.221-222).

The characters in the play ironically confuse temporary illusion for its antithesis, permanent truth. Although Lysander
loves Hermia at both the beginning and the end of the play, in
the middle of the play he hates her with a vehemence that is
utterly certain and inflexible. "Ay, by my life!," Lysander swears

to her, "be out of hope, of question or doubt:/ Be certain: nothing truer: 'tis no jest/ That I do hate thee and love Helena"
(III.ii.277-281). However, Lysander's certainty, emphatic as it
is, is nevertheless a complete delusion that is ultimately proven
false. And despite his passionate vows of faithful devotion to
Helena, his love for her is temporary and is also proven false.
These reversals of perception validate Bassanio's canny ob-
servation, that "outward shows be least themselves."

Like *The Merchant of Venice, A Midsummer Night's Dream*
illustrates that the distinction between extreme opposites—
short and tall, love and hate, night and day—is not absolute in
itself; more important is the interpretive paradigm of the observer, which can transpose any quality to its antithesis. Extreme opposites can easily be confused for one another because the distinction between them is not as significant as the
perspective of the person who perceives them; perceptual paradigm defines value. Like *The Merchant of Venice, A Midsummer Night's Dream* summarizes these issues in its final act,
which is given over to the play-within-a-play performed by
the "rude mechanicals."

The oxymora that describe the dramatic performance
planned for the Duke "on [as Peter Quince says] his wedding-
day at night" (I.ii.7) are a symptom of the convergence and
confusion of extreme opposites that is typical of inverse irony.
The Duke is intrigued by what is advertised as "A tedious brief
scene of young Pyramus/ and his love Thisby: very tragical
mirth" (III.i.56-57). "Merry and tragical! tedious and brief!,"
he exclaims. "That is hot ice and wondrous strange snow. How
shall we find the concord of this discord?" (III.i.58-60).

Similar to the bright moonlight that appears to be "day-light
sick" in act five of *The Merchant of Venice*, the moonlight in
the Pyramus and Thisby play is bright enough to be confused
for day. "Sweet Moon," the misguided Pyramus says:

I thank thee for thy sunny beams;

> I thank thee, Moon, for shining now so bright;
> For, by thy gracious, golden, glittering [gleams],
> I trust to take of truest Thisby sight.   (*MND*, V.i.276-280)

In the role of Pyramus, Bottom confuses the deceptive moon-light for its antithesis, "sunny beams." And although Pyramus by moonlight trusts to be "of truest Thisby sight," he mistakenly concludes that Thisby is dead, when in fact she is alive. The moon appears to be as bright as day, but nevertheless, the apparent clarity of vision is a delusion. Pyramus believes what he sees because he does not have Bassanio's sophistication to know that what appears to be true is in fact least likely to be true.

The play-within-a-play puts Lysander and Hermia, Demetrius and Helena into the role of audience, giving them the opportunity to see clearly and laugh at the confusion of opposites that is analogous to what their own situation had been just a short while previously. As characters, they had been blind to the inverse irony of their own situation, but as the audience within the play, they can see clearly the irony in the country bumpkins' situation. As the characters watch the play-within-a play, they represent "audience" in microcosm, even as they necessarily remain blind to the irony that they continue to be characters in a play watching a play. The implication of this chain of analogy is that we, as an audience, are similarly blind to the irony of our own lives, even as we presume to see quite clearly the ironies that confuse the characters in a play. But we forget that the chain of analogy extends full circle, from the stage as a microcosm of the world to the world itself as a stage, where mankind plays a variety of roles and can be as blind to the ironies of life as characters in a comedy.

The play-within-a-play establishes an equivalence by analogy between actors and audience, thereby eroding the distinction between art and life, fantasy and reality, appearance and truth. In this context, truth is not absolute, but is relative to perspective, a point that the play-within-a-play exemplifies. The Pyramus and Thisbe story is neither tragic nor comic in itself: its meaning is defined by interpretive paradigm—by perspective and context. The Pyramus and Thisbe story is tragic in Chaucer and Ovid, but it is hilarious when performed by Bottom, Peter Quince and the others—even though the basic facts of the story remain the same. Just as Portia had explained in her discussion of candles and moonlight in act five of *The Merchant of Venice*, framework of perspective defines meaning—and a radical shift in interpretive paradigm can invert that meaning.

The Pyramus and Thisbe story represents a convergence of opposites; it is simultaneously tragic and comic— "very tragical-mirth" that is "tedious-brief." The similarity between "Pyramus and Thisbe" and *Romeo and Juliet* exemplifies the same point. In both stories, the male commits suicide because he mistakenly believes that his female beloved is already dead; she then discovers that he is dead, and subsequently kills herself. In both stories, a mistaken premise is at the root of the tragedy, which conceivably could have been averted if the male had not been so certain that appearance was in fact true to reality, prompting the mistaken-but-unshakable belief that his beloved had died. The basic facts are similar, but can be perceived as opposite antitheses according to the lights of shifting paradigms. Shakespeare gives the Pyramus and Thisbe story a comic treatment in *A Midsummer Night's Dream*, while he gives a tragic treatment to *Romeo and Juliet.*

Despite the various conflicts between extreme opposites within *Romeo and Juliet* (love versus hate, Montague versus Capulet), the play is fundamentally a tragedy of misperception, based on the mistaken perception of opposites. Romeo meets Juliet because an illiterate messenger does not recognize that he is a Montague, and asks him to read the invitation to the

Capulet's ball. Romeo commits suicide because extreme op-posites—life and death—have a similar appearance; he con-fuses the appearance of death—Juliet's deep sleep—for death itself. Friar Laurence's letter might have helped him to reframe Juliet's apparent death in terms of life. But since words and language cannot keep pace with the rapid speed of violent emotion, the Friar's letter does not arrive in time to prevent Romeo's suicide—an error that might have been prevented. Romeo's servant, Balthasar, who brings Romeo the misinfor-mation that Juliet is dead, had warned him to restrain his emotions: "I do beseech you, sir, have patience./ Your looks are pale and wild, and do import some misadventure" (V.ii.29). Romeo, however, is certain—with the full-force of all his emo-tion—that outward appearances are true. "Tush, thou art de-ceived" (V.ii.30) he says to Balthasar, unaware that he is the one who has been deceived.

In act three, at the mid-point of the play—when the play's opposite extremes (beginning and end) are equidistant—Shakespeare brings into grand focus the convergence and con-fusion of antithetical opposites: marriage and murder, love and hate, day and night. It is notable that Romeo marries Juliet and murders Tybalt at virtually the same moment. The com-mon identity of these two opposite extremes—murder and marriage—is evident from the order of events. The wedding ceremony comes first. Mortal combat comes second. And the consummation of the marriage comes third. Tybalt's bleeding from Romeo's sword is analogous to the bleeding that takes place when Romeo breaks Juliet's maidenhead; this juxtapo-sition of opposites recalls the bloody-bawdy punning in act one (I.i.27-31).

It is also notable that Romeo had been trying to act as a peace-maker, and that the death of Tybalt was a result that was con-trary to his original intention. Romeo had wanted to show love to Tybalt, who had become his kinsman following his mar-

riage to Juliet. But when Romeo attempted to quell the fight
between Mercutio and Tybalt, he inadvertently enables Tybalt
to kill Mercutio; and then kills Tybalt in revenge. Romeo had
meant to stop their fight, but instead his actions result in the
deaths of both men.

Juliet's reaction to these events—her marriage to Romeo,
Romeo's murder of Tybalt—is full of oxymora that express the
convergence of extreme opposites. In the interim between her
wedding and the consummation of her marriage, she learns
about Tybalt's murder and tries to reconcile this violent act
with her loving image of Romeo:

> O serpent heart, hid with a flow'ring face!
> Did ever dragon keep so fair a cave?
> Beautiful tyrant! fiend angelical!
> Dove-feather'd raven, wolvish ravening lamb!
> Despised substance of divinest show!
> Just opposite to what thou justly seem'st—
> A damned saint, an honourable villain!
> O nature, what hadst thou to do in hell
> When thou didst bower the spirit of a fiend
> In mortal paradise of such sweet flesh?
> Was ever book containing such vile matter
> So fairly bound? O that deceit should dwell
> In such a gorgeous palace!   (III.ii.72-85)

Juliet echoes *A Midsummer Night's Dream*'s juxtaposition of
ravens and doves, an inversion of black and white. Similar to
Bassanio's speech on outward shows in act three of *The Merchant of Venice*, she elucidates the principle of inverse irony,
which in this context is tragic rather than festive: "Despised
substance of divinest show, / Just opposite to what thou justly
seem'st—"

As Juliet tries to reconcile ambivalent emotions, she tells
herself that the difference between opposites—love and hate—
is a matter of perspective. The countervailing balance between
antithetical opposites is evident in her line of reasoning: "My
husband lives, that Tybalt would have slain, / And Tybalt's dead

that would have slain my husband: / all this is comfort; where-fore weep I then?" (III.ii.105-108).

Ambiguous language complements the ambivalence of in-tense emotion, enabling Juliet to disguise her feelings from her mother while speaking honestly—though ironically—of her love for Romeo.

> **Lady Capulet**: Thou weep'st not so much for his [Tybalt's] death,
> As that villain lives which slaughtered him....
> **Juliet**: Ay, madam, from the reach of these my hands.
> Would none but I might venge my cousin's death! (III.V.79-87)

There is a double irony here. Lady Capulet does not suspect Juliet's love for Romeo—and Juliet does not realize the extent to which she will in fact revenge her cousin's death, achieving through her love for Romeo the same result that Lady Capulet's hatred would have intended for him. Juliet (who loves Romeo) is responsible for his death, while Lady Capulet (who hates Romeo) fails in her attempt to have him poisoned. Intense love and intense hatred—supposedly extreme opposites—are equally destructive and ultimately achieve the same result. Like Romeo who was responsible for the deaths of Tybalt and Mercutio when he had meant to stop their fighting, both Juliet and her mother bring about consequences that are contrary to their original intention, which is further proof of the ines-capable fact that supposedly extreme opposites—violent love and violent hate—are more similar than different.

As in *A Midsummer Night's Dream* and *The Merchant of Venice*, Shakespeare uses the metaphors day and night, the brightness of the sun and the blackness of ravens' feathers to explore the issues of inverse irony, interpretive paradigm and the similarity and inversion of opposites. Juliet identifies Romeo with the night; and then asserts that he is like a "day in night" that can outshine the sun in beauty:

Come, night; come Romeo; come thou day in night,

For thou wilt lie upon the wings of night,
Whiter than new snow [on] a raven's back.
Give me my Romeo; and, when [he] shall die,
Take him and cut him out in little stars,
And he will make the face of heaven so fine
That all the world will be in love with night
And pay no worship to the garish sun.   (III.ii.17-25)

From Juliet's perspective, powerful emotion—love—has the power to invert night and day. Alive, Romeo is the day that overpowers night. Dead, he is the night that overpowers day. Her metaphor is a poetic restatement of the principle of inverse irony that is so fundamental to the festive logic of *The Merchant of Venice*—that outward show is least itself. To quote once more Juliet's formulation of Bassanio's principle: "Despised substance of divinest show!/ Just opposite to what thou justly seem'st—" (III.ii.77-78).

Similarly, Romeo's intense love for Juliet also inverts night and day. As Romeo gazes at the stars, he imagines Juliet's eyes shining as she looks into the black of night:

What if her eyes were there [in the sky], they [the stars] in her head?
The brightness of her cheek would shame those stars,
As daylight doth a lamp; her eyes in heaven
Would through the airy region stream so bright,
That birds would sing and think it were not night.   (II.ii.15-22)

As in Portia's parable of the bright moonlight and the light of the candle, the more powerful light overpowers a lesser light, in this case "as daylight doth a lamp." And light, a metaphor for man's ability to perceive reality, can invert opposite extremes, such as day and night.

A logical consequence of this type of thinking is the corollary that extreme opposites converge to a point of common identity, either in oxymoron (where both contrary elements are visible) or in gross deceptiveness (where one element is hidden by its extreme opposite). Therefore Juliet calls Romeo "A damned saint, an honourable villain!" (III.ii.79). In this context, day and night resemble each other enough to be confused for one another.

When Capulet sends his wife to inform Juliet that she will marry the man of his choice (Paris) in three days, it is "so very late, that we/ May call it early by and by" (III.iv.34-35). When Lady Capulet arrives at Juliet's room, Juliet responds to her mother in words that mirror Capulet's: "Is she not down so late, or up so early?" (III.v.67). At this point in time, Juliet has consummated her marriage with Romeo, who has just departed at that late hour of twilight when extremely late night and extremely early morning converge, when it is impossible to differentiate day from night. His parting was occasion for extended metaphor of inverted opposites. Juliet had said to Romeo:

> Wilt thou be gone? It is not yet near day.
> It was the nightingale, and not the lark,
> That pierced the fearful hollow of thine ear.
> Nightly she sings on yond pomegranate tree.
> Believe me, love, it was the nightingale.
> **Romeo:** It was the lark, the herald of the morn,
> No nightingale...
> **Juliet:** Yond light is not daylight, I know it, I;
> It is some meteor that the sun exhales
> To be to thee this night a torch-bearer....
> **Romeo:** I am content, so thou wilt have it so.
> I'll say yon grey is not the morning's eye,
> 'Tis but the pale reflex of Cynthia's brow;
> Nor that is not the lark, whose notes do beat
> The vaulty heaven so high above our heads.
> I have more care to stay than will to go.
> Come, death, and welcome! Juliet wills it so.
> How is't, my soul? Let's talk; it is not day.
> **Juliet:** It is, it is! Hie hence, be gone, away!
> It is the lark that sings so out of tune,
> Straining harsh discords and unpleasing sharps.
> Some say the lark makes sweet division;
> This doth not so, for she divideth us.
> Some say the lark and loathed toad change eyes;
> O' now I would they had chang'd voices too...
> **Romeo:** More light and light; more dark and dark our woes!

(III.v.1-36)

Like Portia, who had spoken of the relative beauty of the lark's song, Romeo and Juliet understand that any simple fact of nature—the time of day, for example—is just itself, without any inherent ambiguity. "Wherefore art thou Romeo?....," Juliet asks. "That which we call a rose/ by any other name would smell as sweet" (II.ii.33-44). However, they also understand that man perceives reality through the filter of perceptual paradigms that inevitably impose upon nature a contradictory ambiguity. The same bird song is either a lark or a nightingale, depending upon one's point of view. Likewise the song of the lark: it is out of tune because Juliet's emotional state colors it so. Similarly, the time of day: it is both day and night simultaneously or one or the other, depending upon the perspective that Romeo and Juliet define for it.

Romeo and Juliet demonstrates on every level the essential identity of ostensible opposites. The Montagues and Capulets are extreme opposites in the sense that they are in mortal combat with one another; but they are similar in that they are hotblooded, violent people. They believe themselves to be opposites, but ironically, they are blind to their essential likeness, which is obvious both to the audience and to the people of Verona who are not personally involved with them in their quarrels—a likeness that is the basis for the love that blossoms between Romeo and Juliet.

Romeo and Juliet's love is commonly believed to stand out in contrast to their families' hatred. But murder and marriage complement one another in Romeo, who is buffeted by impulsive passion—both love and hate. Likewise, Romeo and Juliet's love complements their families' hatred, counterbalancing passionate love and passionate hatred—two extreme opposites that prove to be more similar than different. As René Girard says:

> All our theories of conflict and even our language reflect the common-sense view that the more intense the conflict, the wider the

separation between the antagonists. The tragic spirit operates on the opposite principle: the more intense the conflict, the less room for difference in it.[195]

Romeo and Juliet's passionate love and their families' passionate hatred are fundamentally identical. Montagues and Capulets kill each other out of hatred; Romeo and Juliet kill themselves out of love. The end result of their violent passion is that the lovers die and fighters live in harmony.

The tragedy of *Romeo and Juliet* is complementary to the comedy of *A Midsummer Night's Dream*: both are rich in examples of inverse irony, in which extreme opposites are repeatedly mistaken for one another. Both are rich in oxymora, the literary convergence of opposites; both are filled with metaphors of inverted opposites and puns that play upon antithetical meanings. They tell a story of misread messages, mistaken identities and fervently deluded passions. These plays repeatedly demonstrate that appearance can be least itself. Taken together, the two plays illustrate a corollary of inverse irony, that opposites can be identical, that tragedy and comedy are identical opposites—opposite sides to a single coin. The complementary relationship between these two plays demonstrates that the irreducible facts of life can be either tragic or comic, depending upon the paradigm according to which those facts are interpreted.

People are accustomed to perceiving in Shakespeare plays themes that are defined as a conflict between binary opposites—in the parlance of nineteenth-century German dialectical philosophy, as thesis versus antithesis; for example, the conflict between opposite extremes such as love versus hate, Jew versus Christian, comedy versus tragedy, black versus white. However, the meaning of Shakespearean drama seems to lie in a higher level perspective, a synthesis that stands above the conflict between thesis and antithesis, a perspective that does not sympathize with either of these conflicting points of view, but stands at an ironic distance from both, perceiving a structural balance and moral equivalence between ostensibly opposite extremes.[196] In these terms, issues related to Christian/Jewish conflict in *The Merchant of Venice*—mercy versus revenge, for example—represent the clash between thesis and antithesis, while Shakespeare's meaning lies in the synthesis, a detached, ironic view from above that sees an equivalence between warring opposites, and does not prefer one side to the other. Christian and Jewish values are equally wrong, from the perspective of ancient Roman honor.

The principle of inverse irony, the inversion of extreme opposites and other related issues recur in other Shakespeare plays. In *Much Ado About Nothing*, Beatrice and Benedick engage in a "merry war" (I.i.62)—a "skirmish of wit" (I.i.64)—that signifies the convergence of love and hate. Expressing his disdain for Beatrice, Benedick says to Don Pedro, the prince of Arragon:

> Will your grace command me any service to the world's end? I will go on the slightest errand now to the Antipodes that you can devise to send me on.....rather than hold three words' conference with this harpy.   (II.i.271-280)

In saying that he'd rather go "on the slightest errand...to the Antipodes," Benedick expresses in the strongest possible terms his antipathy for Beatrice. But this sentiment, like Benedick's emphatic resolve never to marry (I.i.239-270) is very promptly reversed completely.

Benedick's relationship with Beatrice blossoms when he decides to interpret outward show as least itself, such that he hears affection when she spews sarcasm. "'Against my will I am sent to bid you come in to dinner,'" he says to himself, thinking over Beatrice's seemingly rude words of invitation. Nevertheless, contrary to all external evidence of her rudeness, he believes that "there's some double meaning in that [her petulant words]." He considers possible reasons why

Beatrice's sour attitude could be interpreted as sweet (II.iii.266-268).

Paradoxically, Benedick becomes predisposed to discount outward show because he has been deceived by superficial appearance. His friends stage a mock-serious discussion that they intend for him to overhear, ostensibly talking among themselves about Beatrice's love for him. Benedick is taken in by this deception because he accepts superficial appearance at face value: "This can be no trick," he says of his friends' charade, "the conference was sadly bourne" (*Ado*, II.iii.228-229). In other words, the discussion appeared to be serious; therefore it must have been sincere. After that, he perceives Beatrice from a perceptual paradigm of love, rather than disdain, and he perceives even her sharpest sarcasm as affectionate.

Complementary to the good-humored trick played upon Benedick by his friends is the mean-spirited deception of Claudio by his enemy, Don John, who manipulates outward appearance to turn Claudio against his fiancée, Hero. Deceived by appearance, Benedick plans to marry Beatrice; deceived by appearance, Claudio turns against Hero, insulting and humiliating her at what would have been their wedding ceremony, which he cuts short with accusations of infidelity. Benedick's love and Claudio's betrayal are both based upon misleading appearance, which both take at face value. Though the results are contrary, both Benedick and Claudio have made the same mistake. Benedick's friends and Claudio's enemies have perpetrated a similar deception. The two deeds are identical/opposites.

In contrast to the aristocratic Benedick and Claudio, the comic constable Dogberry routinely takes everything in a manner contrary to appearance. He mistakenly refers to the defendants as the plaintiffs (V.1.261); he identifies himself and his partner as the malefactors (IV.ii.3-4), when the criminals—not the constable—should be considered the malefactors. But even though he works from assumptions that are inverted, Dogberry is the one who manages to set the world right again for the aristocrats who were blind to reality because they assumed that words correspond to their presumed meaning, and that the outward appearance of truth corresponds to the actual truth.

Like Benedick, Petruchio in *The Taming of the Shrew* courts his wife in a merry war, although the balance between "merry" and "war" tilts more to war than in Benedick's battle of wits with Beatrice, which is more genteel. Like Benedick, who found a sweet and gentle message in Beatrice's rude and sarcastic dinner invitation, Petruchio persists in perceiving Kate's anger and sarcasm as its opposite—gentleness and kindness—despite all superficial evidence to the contrary. However, while Benedick has been deceived into misinterpreting Beatrice's sarcasm for affection, Petruchio—like Bassanio—follows a calculated strategy to arrive at a financially advantageous marriage. Kate's money is the determining factor in how Petruchio chooses to perceive her. His courtship of Kate stands upon the premise that outward show is least itself: Although her exterior (that is, her shrewish manner) may be of lead (to speak in the parlance of the caskets), Petruchio looks beyond outward show to the gold that is within—the gold that is her fortune. No doubt he had heard only reports of Kate's shrewishness. But he comes courting her as if she were "fair and virtuous" (II.i.43):

> I am a gentleman of Verona, sir
> That hearing of her beauty and her wit,
> Her affability and bashful modesty,
> Her wondrous qualities and mild behavior,
> Am bold to show myself a forward guest
> Within your house, to make mine eye the witness
> Of that report which I so oft have heard...   (II.i.47-53)

Of course he's lying. He has heard the exact opposite to the compliments and praise for Kate that he says he has heard, and he will completely discount the proof of Kate's shrewishness that his eyes will soon witness. After his first skirmish with her—both verbal and physical—Petruchio tells Kate, contrary to all evidence, that he finds her "passing gentle" (II.i.244).

'Twas told me you were rough and coy and sullen
And now I find report a very liar;
For thou art pleasant, gamesome, passing courteous,
But slow in speech, yet sweet as spring-time flowers.
Thou canst not frown, thou canst not look askance,
Nor bite thy lip, as angry wenches will,
Nor hast thou pleasure to be cross in talk,
But thou with mildness entertain'st thy wooers,
With gentle conference, soft and affable.
Why does the world report that Kate doth limp?
O sland'rous world! Kate like the hazel-twig
Is straight and slender, and as brown in hue
As hazel nuts and sweeter than the kernels.
O, Let me see thee walk. Thou dost not halt.   (II.i.245-258)

Like Titania, who sees the jackass-headed Bottom as beautiful and graceful, Petruchio's affection runs contrary to all outward evidence. However, his perception hasn't been affected by fairy dust, like the characters in *A Midsummer Night's Dream*. It is more likely gold dust that has caused him to see the world in a manner contrary to superficial appearance.

Petruchio is determined to perceive Kate on his own terms, contrary to how the rest of the world sees her. He is not at all intimidated by the "facts" of her appearance. He does not hesitate to tell the world—just as he has told Kate—that hot is cold, temper is temperance, sarcasm is affection:

If she be curst, it is for policy
For she's not froward, but modest as the dove;
She is not hot, but temperate as the morn;
For patience she will prove a second Grissel,
And Roman Lucrece for her chastity...   (II.i.294-298)

Like Benedick, he concludes that sarcasm is sweetness, substituting one extreme for another because both are relative to his perception.

When Kate publicly and vehemently states her opposition to Petruchio's intention to marry her, he calmly explains to all assembled that appearance is antithetical to reality. "Be patient, gentlemen," he advises, knowing—as Romeo did not—that without patience, one reacts emotionally (and therefore mistakenly) to apparent facts (which only appear to be true.) "'Tis a bargain'd twixt us twain, being alone," he says, "That she shall still be curst in company" (II.i.304-307).

Petruchio's "taming" of Kate is a rigorous training in inverse irony. She says the food at their wedding feast is good; but contrary to Kate's opinion, which is based on the actual taste of the food, Petruchio says the banquet food is bad and throws it out (IV.ii.164-174). He deprives her of food, rest, comfort and sleep "under the name of perfect love" (IV.iii.12). She perceives the gown and cap as fashionable—clothing that "doth fit the time/ And gentlewomen wear such caps as these" (IV.iii.69-70). But Petruchio's truth runs contrary to the dictates of fashion; he does not make any concession to conventional judgments of value. He berates the haberdasher, denigrates the fashionable clothes and destroys them, all the while insisting to Kate that appearance doesn't matter:

> Our purses shall be proud, our garments poor,
> For 'tis the mind that makes the body rich;
> And as the sun breaks through the darkest clouds
> So honour peereth in the meanest habit.
> What, is the jay more precious than the lark,
> Because the feathers are more beautiful?
> Or is the adder better than the eel,
> Because his painted skin contents the eye?
> Oh, no, good Kate; neither art thou the worse
> For this poor furniture and mean array.
> If thou account's it shame, lay it on me;
> And therefore frolic.   (IV.iii.173-184)

Like Bassanio in *The Merchant of Venice*, Petruchio articulates a lofty perspective according to which mere appearance is not what matters. At one level, it is a noble sentiment that he expresses, though at another level, he only cares about the money. Like Bassanio, Petruchio is simultaneously idealistic and self-serving, sincere and hypocritical, truthful and deceptive.

Petruchio brings Kate's taming to a climax when he asserts the ultimate in inverse irony, that even the time of day is not an indisputable fact, but is subject to his self-determined perception of the hour. When Petruchio says it is seven o'clock, Kate contradicts him, saying that it is "almost two" (IV.iii.191). "It shall be seven ere I go to horse...," he replies. "It shall be what o'clock I say it is" (IV.iii.193-197). To which Hortensio says: "Why, so this gallant will command the sun" (IV.iv.198)—which is precisely the point.

In the famous exchange on the road to his father-in-law's house, Petruchio says: "Good Lord, how bright and goodly shines the moon!" Kate replies:

> The moon! The sun. It is not moonlight now.
> **Petruchio:** I say it is the moon that shines so bright.
> **Kate:** I know it is the sun that shines so bright.
> **Petruchio:** Now, by my mother's son, and that's myself,
> It shall be moon, or star, or what I list,
> Or ere I journey to your father's house.—...
> **Kate:** Forward, I pray, since we have come so far,
> And be it the moon, or sun, or what you please
> An if you please to call it a rush-candle,
> Henceforth I vow it shall be so for me.
> **Petruchio:** I say it is the moon.
> **Kate:** I know it is the moon.
> **Petruchio:** Nay, then you lie; it is the blessed sun.
> **Kate:** Then, God be bless'd, it is the blessed sun;
> But sun it is not, when you say it is not;
> And the moon changes even as your mind.
> What you will have it nam'd, even that it is;
> And so it shall be so for Katherine.   (IV.v.2-22)

Here Petruchio challenges the epistemological foundation of medieval thought, usurping God's divine prerogative to name the bright light the "sun" and the lesser light the "moon." If man himself determines the meaning of words, then God's word is likewise relative to man's perspective and therefore in doubt—along with the entire Great Chain of Being, the religious worldview based on what is presumed to be the absolute truth of the Bible. Relative truth and absolute truth are incompatible opposites.

Petruchio is antithetical to the lovers in *A Midsummer Night's Dream* and *Romeo and Juliet* in so far as his judgment is not clouded by emotion. He certainly knows the difference between day and night, the sun and the moon, two o'clock and seven o'clock. Nevertheless, just as Romeo and Juliet could banter about whether it is dawn or dusk, the lark or the nightingale, Petruchio and Kate argue over whether it is the sun or the moon that is overhead. Like Portia, Petruchio understands that truth is relative to perspective, which can blur the distinction between bright moonlight or pale daylight. Appearance, as such, could well be contrary to reality. Opposite extremes might well be so similar in appearance that the difference between them might be nothing more than an arbitrary act of will. Petruchio knows, like Shakespeare himself, that he can make night into day, if he so wishes; he is the master of his own destiny because he understands that he personally is the measure of truth as he sees it; he can portray reality in any manner that he wishes. Reality might be as arbitrary as a personal whim, but since it is determined by an act of will, it could also be as constant and consistent as a personal promise would be according to ancient Roman honor.

The Merchant of Venice is similar to other Shakespeare plays in which Shakespeare employs his artistry to demonstrate that the correspondence between the appearance of truth and truth itself is by no means certain. The principle of inverse irony, so important to the honor/irony interpretation of *The Merchant of Venice*, is a consistent thread that runs through at least a half-dozen plays. The honor/irony interpretation of the play, then, is based on a theme that falls within the mainstream of Shakespeare's work. To be sure, other Shakespeare plays are not as cryptic as *The Merchant of Venice* has proven to be over the centuries. But *The Merchant of Venice* is the exception that proves the importance of the rule—that outward show is least itself. In contrast, a play that is construed to be Shakespeare's only work of Christian apologetics would be simply an exception to the rule, a caveat that is conceded even by those who believe the play to be an example of Christian apologetics.[197]

Suggestions for performance

A performance of *The Merchant of Venice* based on the honor/irony interpretation must use a variety of means to dissociate perception of the play from conventional preconceptions. The objective is twofold: first, to disrupt the audience's preconceived notions; and second, to communicate the paradox that an antithetical reality is hidden behind every ostensible reality. Portia and the other characters in this play must be shown to have two faces: one the ostensible face of honor; the other, the actual face of comic irony.

For these reasons, it would be helpful to avoid traditional Shakespearean garb and accent. A fresh cultural context can help an audience to see a traditional text in a new light. Contemporary cultural cues (in clothing and conversational style) can bring the play's message directly to the audience on the audience's own terms; archaic conventions play into preconceptions about Shakespeare and *The Merchant of Venice*.

In addition, reverse type-casting (that is, reverse in terms of how the play has been usually cast) is an approach that could also be used to disrupt audience preconceptions. For example, Shylock's appearance should contradict every possible Jewish stereotype. He should be tall, blond and handsome, played by an aristocratic, Gentile-type—no skullcaps, scraggly beards, side-curls or Yiddish accent. He should be impressively forceful, cold, contemptuous and restrained in his passion, not hot tempered and volcanic. But despite his aristocratic bearing, he should be dressed shabbily to the point of clownishness to heighten the contrast with his towering personal dignity. In short, a noble Roman in a comic mask.

Lancelot Gobbo, the clown, is the character who can be played as Jewish stereotype, with a heavy Yiddish accent—not Shylock. His puns and word play should sound like the Jewish humor that parodies Talmudic rationality, in which the meaning of a word or phrase is analyzed to the point of absurdity. Lancelot should be similar in some respects to Jewish comedians such as Jackie Mason or Jerry Seinfeld.

Like Shylock, Jessica should not look Jewish in any way. Her physical appearance should be glamorous, like a fashion model. However, she should look strongly masculine when she escapes from home in disguise on the night of the masque, when she should wear a large cod piece. Lorenzo, in contrast, should be disguised in drag when he comes to help Jessica escape on the night of the masque. Jessica should always appear to be the dominant partner in the relationship: when they are in disguise, she appears to be bigger and stronger; when they are not in disguise, she is stunningly tall and stunningly beautiful, while he is short and homely.

Antonio should be a pretender to the dignity that Shylock assumes. He might be played like a Damon Runyon character who speaks "educated" English that sounds ignorant, as if the words he uses were somehow beyond his own comprehension. He should also be very grave and dignified, but dressed shabbily in a manner identical to Shylock. They should wear the same ridiculous suit—perhaps plaid, or checked. Their clothes should be laughable, in contrast to their personal bearing, which should be extremely serious. Together they should illustrate the point that outward show—clothes—runs counter to the inner reality of the spirit; and also, that opposite extremes can appear identical. Portia as judge-in-disguise is predisposed to hate Shylock and admire Antonio as the one in whom the ancient Roman honor most appears. However, when she sees them both for the first time, she should be genuinely confused that they should both appear equally ridiculous, saying: "Which is the merchant here? and which the Jew?" (4.1.171).

Bassanio should be a muscle-bound "hunk," as befits a blood relation to Antonio, a literary descendant of Hercules. He should be physically impressive to the point where his muscle-bound magnificence begins to imply mental deficiency. However, his overly-masculine appearance doesn't preclude the possibility that his personality might be slightly effeminate and passive. This hint of homosexuality helps explain Bassanio's interest in the young doctor of Rome, "Balthasar;" and his willingness to give his wedding ring to her/him. His relatively low level of interest in Portia as a woman also reinforces his financial interest in courting her.

Bassanio is a sincere/fake character. He wears up-to-the minute fashions, and looks passé. He utters profundities and sounds superficial. He can be rudely polite in the Steve Martin style—"Well, excuuuuse me!" As a practiced fortune hunter, Bassanio knows how to assume a persona that will impress a wealthy heiress. When courting Portia, he wears contact lenses, an expensive designer suit and a modestly-long head of hair. However, his appearance is completely different when he is with Antonio, when he could be dressed in leather—as a punk rocker—wearing sun glasses, an earring and with tattoos visible. Perhaps his head is shaven, so that what later appears to be a fine head of hair is actually a hair piece.

One thing Bassanio and Portia have in common is that they are both quite different from the appearance they try to project when they are supposed to be "good." Therefore, they are not disappointed when the masks are discarded, and they find that they share a common style and similar attitudes. Portia should be an ambiguous juxtaposition of opposites—a whore/Madonna—who sometimes seems spiritual, sometimes carnal, but always communicates a hint of the contrary characteristic when either spirituality or carnality is dominant. Like Bassanio, Portia should alternate between two persona: one, an aggressive punk rocker type for whom love and money are both euphemisms for sex; the other, a highly refined person of wealth and culture. She should be a cross between Meryl Streep and Madonna, a hybrid of culture and crudity. In her "punk" incarnation, she speaks dreamily and seductively, in a little girl voice that contrasts with her aggressive appearance. In her "refined" incarnation, she should appear elegant in a way that contrasts sharply with the image she initially presents, but her tone of voice should have a hard, cynical edge that gives a false ring to her soft words; her crude tone of voice should contrast with her elegant image.

Portia should have short, closely cropped black hair that suggests a masculine edge to her aggressive sexuality. Her "long blond hair," which has captured Bassanio's imagination, is actually a wig that should be evident in her first scene, in her bedroom on a stand that resembles "poor Yorick" from *Hamlet*. This wig should represent a very elaborate, fashionable hair style; in the style of:

> ... crisped, snaky, golden locks[198]
> Which makes such wanton gambols with the wind
> Upon supposed fairness, often known
> To be the dowry of a second head,
> The skull that bred them in the sepulchre.   (3.2.92-96)

Portia wears this wig when she is formally entertaining suitors in her sophisticated and refined persona. She should wear her own short, black hair when she is disguised as a judge and is supposedly a young man. She wears heavy make-up when she is supposedly herself, but she should appear natural—without make-up—when she is in disguise

In Portia's first scene, chatting privately with Nerissa, her maid, we should see a behind-the-facade glimpse of how Portia really is: She is bored and smoking, possibly marijuana. There should be some drug paraphernalia in the room, perhaps a hookah; as well as anti-drug posters on the wall: "Reefer Madness!" "Just say no!" The anti-drug messages should directly contradict her evident attitude and bearing. The room should look low rent, like a college dormitory. It should contrast sharply with the luxury and style of the drawing room, in which Portia invites her suitors to choose between the caskets.

Portia's disguise as a judge should be fairly superficial, giving Bassanio every opportunity—despite her closely cropped black hair—to recognize her. When she delivers her speech on mercy, spike heels are visible at the hem of her judicial robes. She chews gum and smokes cigarettes simultaneously—behavior that is blatantly unlike that of a judge. Portia tries her best to establish eye contact with Bassanio for a knowing wink, but he doesn't recognize her. She comes on to him in the same manner as she had done in her blond wig, with winks and seductive caresses. But Bassanio is too dense to "get it," even though he would be able to see through Portia's disguise immediately, if he weren't so self-absorbed. Portia should ask Bassanio for her ring in a seductive way, in the spirit of flirting with him. However, Bassanio thinks a man is coming on to him (albeit an androgynous, feminine man)—and he seems to be somewhat interested.

Portia's lascivious nature should be evident by the heavy make-up and revealing clothing that she wears. Venetian women wore platform shoes, bleached their hair, wore heavy make-up ("red with painting, and white with chalke") and wore beautiful clothes.[199] Shylock makes reference to the custom of heavy make-up when he says to Jessica: "Clamber not you up to the casements then, / Nor thrust your head into the public street / To gaze on Christian fools with varnished faces..." (2.5.31-33). Women in white-face with blood-red lips (like Joel Gray in the film *Cabaret*), bleached deathly pale as the bright moonlight, might be blatant in their intent to allure and seduce while having a ghostly aspect—"a second head...in the sepulchre"—lurking behind outward appearances.

"Among Elizabethans," Venice was "a byword for sexual immorality," according to *The Dramatic Use of Bawdy in Shakespeare*.[200] Prostitutes may have been as numerous as 5-to-10 percent of the Venetian population.[201]

> Unfortunately for Venice's respectable women, the city's reputation for sexual license rubbed off, to some extent, on them....They did not help matters when they adopted—doubtless with the tacit consent of the husbands, be it noted—a peculiar fashion in clothing: bare, or nearly bare, breasts in public, on which cosmetics were worn.[202]

One observer of the Venetian scene from the 1590s noted that this fashion was unique to the women of Venice, and was not a style fashionable in Rome, Milan, Naples, or other Italian cities: "Other dames of Italy are much more modest in this regard, for ... they do not uncover their breasts."[203] In short, Portia should look and act like a whore, suggestive of the carnal self-indulgence characteristic of the Roman carnival and the image of Venice in Shakespeare's day as "the pleasure capital of Europe."[204]

In act five, the women of Belmont should appear in white face, as pale as the bright moonlight, with red-apple cheeks, like porcelain-doll strumpets. Appropriate to act five's bawdy dialogue about Bassanio and Graziano's alleged infidelity, the women should wear extremely revealing décolletage, perhaps to the point of being bare-breasted, as in Renaissance Venice. They should also be heavily made-up. When Portia threatens to sleep with the judge who took her ring, it should be obvious from her "cheap" appearance that she would not hesitate to sleep with a man who is not her husband. However, each of the women wears a large crucifix in her extreme décolletage, emphasizing a convergence of carnality and spirituality. The scene should have a nightmarish/dreamlike atmosphere; it should be festive/sepulchral.

Act five is an opportunity to make a very stark statement that the world is topsy-turvy. It takes place in Belmont, Portia's estate, under the light of a full moon that is so bright that it appears to be daylight. The apparent reversal of night for day—it appears to be day, but is actually a very bright night—is a metaphor for the honor/irony interpretation of the play. Shakespeare's verbal description of this situation is clear. As Nerissa says, "when the moon shone, we did not see the candle" (5.1.92). To be sure, the set should include the largest, full moon anyone has seen. However, a well-lit stage with a large, full moon in the background may not communicate a striking reversal of perspective. Consequently, here's where some fairly bizarre reversals might be considered. For example, the moon could appear bright, but yet leave the stage in darkness. Portia's candlestick glows in the dark, but the flame emits no light. The actors could be black lighted, luminescent in white clothing and in white-face against a dark background, as if they were walking photo negatives. White face would also give them a corpse-like appearance, reminiscent of Bassanio's vow: "When this ring / Parts from this finger," Bassanio had said, "then parts life from hence. / O, then be bold to say Bassanio's dead. (3.2.183-185).

Endnotes

1 Except where noted, all line references to *The Merchant of Venice* are to the Oxford Shakespeare edition, ed. Jay L. Halio (New York: Oxford University Press, 1994).

2 W.R. Elton, "Shakespeare and the thought of his age," in *The Cambridge Companion to Shakespeare Studies*, ed. Stanley Wells (Cambridge: Cambridge Univ. Press, 1986), p. 17.

3 David Remnick, writing in *The New Yorker*, Nov. 20, 1995, p. 68.

4 Remnick, p. 80.

5 *The Western Canon: The Books and School of the Ages* (New York: Harcourt Brace & Co., 1994), pp. 3-4.

6 *The Western Canon*, pp. 3-4.

7 *The Merchant of Venice*, first published in a quarto edition in 1600, is about to reach the milestone of its four-hundredth anniversary. Although the exact date of the play's first performance is unknown, scholars believe its stage debut was sometime in the mid- to late-1590s, most likely between 1596 and 1597. See Halio's introduction to the Oxford Shakespeare edition of the play, pp. 27-29 and 59-60. Also see p. xxvii in the editor's introduction to the Arden edition of the play, *The Merchant of Venice*, ed. John Russell Brown, 7th rev. ed. (London: Methuen, 1961).

8 Quotations from Shakespeare plays other than *The Merchant of Venice* are taken from The New Cambridge edition, *The Complete Plays and Poems of William Shakespeare*, ed. William Allan Neilson and Charles Jarvis Hill (Boston: Houghton Mifflin Co., 1970).

9 Plutarch, Shakespeare's source for *Julius Caesar,* provides more detail on Portia's suicide: Portia "took hot burning coals, and cast them into her mouth, and kept her mouth so close, that she choked her self," according to "The Life of Brutus," trans. by Sir Thomas North in *Selected Lives from the Lives of the Noble Grecians and Romans*, Vol. 2, ed. Paul Turner (Carbondale, Ill.: Southern Illinois University Press, 1963), p. 196. The translation, from James Amyot's French translation of Plutarch's original Greek text, was the edition of Plutarch that Shakespeare utilized.

10 Thomas S. Kuhn, *The Structure of Scientific Revolutions* (Chicago: University of Chicago Press, second edition, 1970), International Encyclopedia of Unified Science, 2, No. 2, pp. 174-175.

11 Kuhn, p. 175.

12 Kuhn, p. 6.

13 Kuhn, p. viii.

14 Kuhn, pp. viii-ix.

15 Professor Harold Bloom writes: "Criticism is the art of knowing the hidden roads that go from poem to poem." See *The Anxiety of Influence: A Theory of Poetry* (London: Oxford Univ. Press, 1975), p. 96.

16 Harry Levin, "An Introduction to Coriolanus," *Shakespeare and the Revolution of the Times: Perspectives and Commentaries* (Oxford: Oxford University Press, 1976), p. 190. This article is a reprint of Levin's introduction to the Pelican edition of *Coriolanus* (Baltimore: Penguin Books, 1957).

17 Peter Levi, *The Life and Times of William Shakespeare* (New York: Henry Holt & Co., 1988), pp. 29-30. See also A.L. Rowse, *William Shakespeare: A Biography* (New York: Harper & Row, 1963), p. 35: "At about seven, having learnt to read and write, a boy was ready to enter grammar school, where the whole of one's education was based on Latin." And Marchette Chute, *Shakespeare of London* (New York: E.P. Dutton & Co., 1949), p. 15: "The purpose of schools in the Middle Ages was to turn out learned clerks for church positions, and therefore what the little boys of Renaissance England learned was Latin, more Latin and still more Latin."

18 A.L. Rowse, *What Shakespeare Read and Thought* (New York: Coward, McCann & Geoghegan, 1981), pp. 14-15.

19 *Shakespeare's Roman Plays: The Function of Imagery in the Drama* (Cambridge: Harvard Univ. Press, 1963), p. 207.

20 Charney, p. 209.

21 Charney, p. 211.

22 For a representative sample of opinion, see: Louis B. Wright and Virginia A. LaMar, in the editors' introduction to the widely distributed Folger Library edition of the play (New York: Washington Square Press, 1957), pp. viii-xiv; J. Middleton Murry, *Shakespeare* (London: Jonathan Cape, 1936), pp. 188-211; D.J. Palmer, "*The Merchant of Venice*, or the Importance of Being Earnest," in *Shakespearian Comedy*, ed. David Palmer and Malcolm Bradbury, Stratford upon Avon Studies, No. 14 (New York: Crane, Russak & Co., 1972), pp. 97-120; Marvin Felheim, "The Merchant of Venice," *Shakespeare Studies*, 4 (1968), pp. 94-108; Albert Wertheim, "The Treatment of Shylock and Thematic Integrity *in The Merchant of Venice*," *Shakespeare Studies*, 6 (1972), pp. 75-87.

23 For example, Austin C. Dobbins and Roy W. Battenhouse, "Jessica's Morals: A Theological Perspective," *Shakespeare Studies*, 9 (1976), pp. 107-120; Allan Holliday, "Antonio and the Allegory of Salvation," *Shakespeare Studies*, 4 (1968), pp. 109-118; Francis Fergusson, *Trope and Allegory: Themes Common to Dante and Shakespeare* (Athens, Ga.: Univ. of Georgia Press, 1977), pp. 119-122.

24 C.L. Barber, *Shakespeare's Festive Comedy* (Princeton: Princeton Univ. Press, 1959), pp. 184-91.

25 "Biblical Allusion and Allegory in *The Merchant of Venice*," p. 39 in Sylvan Barnet, ed., *Twentieth Century Interpretations of* The Merchant of Venice: *A Collections of Critical Essays* (Englewood Cliffs, N.J.: Prentice-Hall, 1970).

26 John S. Coolidge, "Law and Love in *The Merchant of Venice*," *Shakespeare Quarterly*, 27, No. 3 (Summer 1970), p. 243.

27 Coolidge, p. 243.

28 "The Mature Comedies," in *Early Shakespeare*, Stratford-Upon-Avon Studies, No. 3 (London: Edward Arnold Ltd., 1961), p. 224.

29 A.D. Moody, "An Ironic Comedy," p. 101 in *Twentieth Century Interpretations of* The Merchant of Venice: *A Collections of Critical Essays*. See also A.D. Moody, *Shakespeare:* The Merchant of Venice, Studies in English Literature, No. 21 (Woodbury, N.Y.: Barron, 1964).

30 Harley Granville-Barker, "The Merchant of Venice," *Prefaces to Shakespeare* (Princeton, N.J.: Princeton Univ. Press, 1946), p. 336.

31 "To Entrap the Wisest," in *William Shakespeare's* The Merchant of Venice, ed. Harold Bloom (New York: Chelsea House, 1986), p. 102. Originally published in Literature and Society—Selected Papers from The English Institute, No. 3 (Baltimore: The Johns Hopkins Univ. Press, 1980). Also included in René Girard, *A Theater of Envy: William Shakespeare* (New York: Oxford Univ. Press, 1991).

32 John Lyon, *The Merchant of Venice* (Boston: Twayne Publishers, 1988), p. 10, cites several interpretations of this sort: Norman Rabkin, *Shakespeare and the Problem of Meaning* (Chicago,1981); Ralph Berry, *Shakespeare and the Awareness of the Audience* (London, 1985); A.D. Nuttall, *A New Mimesis: Shakespeare and the Representation of Reality* (London, 1983); and Alexander Legatt, *Shakespeare's Comedies of Love* (London, 1974). Also, see Lyon, pp. 9-28.

33 Keith Geary, "The Nature of Portia's Victory: Turning to Men in *The Merchant of Venice*," in *Shakespeare Survey*, 37, ed. Stanley Wells (Cambridge: Cambridge Univ. Press, 1984), p. 56.

34 James Shapiro, in *Shakespeare and the Jews* (New York: Columbia University Press, 1996), extends the play's Jewish/Christian thematic dichotomies to English culture generally, contending that the conflict between Antonio and Shylock defines an image of the Jew that was widespread in Elizabethan England and important to the English as a negative point of reference in defining their own national identity. Another recent book—Graham Holderness, *William Shakespeare:* The Merchant of Venice (London: Penguin Books, 1993)—is sensitive to late twentieth-century views on gender and race, but retains the traditional framework of antithetical themes derivative of the Christian/Jewish paradigm, as does *Shakespeare: A Life in Drama*, by Stanley Wells (New York: W.W. Norton & Co., 1995), pp. 58-64.

35 Among these was Heinrich Heine. See "Shylock" in *The Poetry and Prose of Heinrich Heine*, ed. Frederick Ewen (New York: Citadel Press, 1948) pp. 673-74. For a recent history of *Merchant of Venice* criticism, with special attention to Shylock, see John Gross, *Shylock: A Legend and Its Legacy* (New York: Simon & Schuster, 1992).

36 Leslie A. Fiedler, in *The Stranger in Shakespeare* (New York: Stein and Day, 1972), is one of the few critics who makes a point of noting that Antonio is identified in the play as an ancient Roman. See pp. 87-88 and p. 132.

37 For the convenience of the reader, Biblical quotations are taken from

the King James version of The Bible (1611). The Geneva Bible (1560), the most important Bible in English translation prior to the King James version, is the version that Shakespeare is most likely to have read. However, The Geneva Bible is not cited here because its archaic spellings are difficult for contemporary readers and, moreover, do not coincide with the spellings of words used in the First Folio. For example, The Geneva Bible spells the word in question above as "Publicane," while both the First Folio and the King James version of the Bible use "publican." Therefore there is little to be gained by citing The Geneva Bible rather than the King James version. Also, in an instance where a word suggests an allusion to the Bible and the word in question is slightly different in the King James and Geneva translations, the First Folio follows the King James translation: e.g., the word "jot" is used in the King James version; "iota" is used in the The Geneva Bible; but *The Merchant of Venice* speaks of "no jot" of blood (MV, 4.1.303), rather than "no iota" of blood. See the chapter below, "The letter of the law and the spirit of love."

38 Professor H.B. Charlton believes "how like a fawning publican" is a displaced line that should be attributed to Antonio. Charlton goes so far as to say that this statement should not even be attributed to Shylock—despite consistent attribution to Shylock in the quartos, the Folio and all modern editions of the play. "It is hardly credible that Shakespeare made Shylock say of Antonio—'How like a fawning publican he looks,'" Charlton writes, commenting that this term "has no apparent application to Antonio, even from Shylock's point of view." See H.B. Charlton, *Shakespearian Comedy* (New York: Barnes & Noble University Paperback, UP 156, n.d., originally published in 1938), pp. 138-39.

39 Plutarch, p. 106: "Now it had been a speech of old time, that the family of the Antonii were descended from one Anton, the son of Hercules, whereof the family took name." Shakespeare follows Plutarch on this point in *Antony and Cleopatra*, where Antony says: "Teach me,/ Alcides [that is, Hercules], thou mine ancestor, thy rage" (IV.xii.43-44).

40 In the the the First Folio edition of *Julius Caesar*, Caesar calls Antony "Antonio" several times: (I.ii.3), (I.ii.4), (I.ii.6), (I.ii.37) and (I.ii.190). In the Folio version of *Antony and Cleopatra*, Cleopatra refers to Antony as "Antonio" twice: (I.v.38) and (II.v.26); Enobarbus calls Antony "Antonio" one time, (II.ii.7). The First Folio is the original source for both *Julius Caesar* and *Antony and Cleopatra,* which—unlike *The Merchant of Venice*—were not published previously in a Quarto edition.

41 See Alan Watson, *Rome of the XII Tables: Persons and Property* (Princeton: Princeton Univ. Press, 1975), pp. 123-24; and Max Radin, "Secare Partis: The Early Roman Law of Execution Against a Debtor," *American Journal of Philology*, 43 (1922), No. 169, pp. 32-48.

42 *Ancient Roman Statutes*, ed. Allan Chester Johnson, et. al. (Austin: Univ. of Texas Press, 1961), p. 10.

43 Friedrich Nietzsche, *Toward a Genealogy of Morals*, trans. Walter

Kaufmann (New York: Random House, 1974), Second Essay, section 5, p. 500.

44 John Russell Brown includes ancient Roman law among possible source material in his preface to the Arden edition of *The Merchant of Venice*, pp.xxvii-xxviii. German legal commentators, in particular, were "interested in the possible derivation of the 'pound of flesh' legend from the law of the Twelve Tables," according to George W. Keeton, *Shakespeare's Legal and Political Background*, (London: Sir Isaac Pitman & Sons Ltd., 1967), p. 149; and pp. 148-150. Also see Owen Hood Phillips, "The Trial in *The Merchant of Venice*," in *Shakespeare and the Lawyers* (London: Methuen, 1972) and Josef Kohler, *Shakespeare vor dem Forum der Jurisprudenz*, second ed. (Berlin: Rotschild, 1919), especially Part I.

45 One notable exception to mainstream criticism is Harris Jay Griston, *Shaking the Dust from Shakespeare* (New York: Cosmopolis, 1924), who contended that *The Merchant of Venice* takes place in the fourth century A.D., at a time when the influence of Christianity was increasing but The Twelve Tables of Rome was still the law of the land. His intent was to show that at this time in history, there was a legal basis for a bond that would take a pound of flesh in the event of forfeiture. This position contrasts with that articulated by Harley Granville-Barker (among others) that: "*The Merchant of Venice* is a fairy tale. There is no more reality in Shylock's bond and the Lord of Belmont's will than in Jack and the Beanstalk" (*Prefaces to Shakespeare*, p. 335). Although Griston emphasizes the link between Shylock's bond and Roman law, he does not go beyond the themes of the traditional Christian/Jewish interpretive paradigm. Instead, his interpretation of the play is reductive to a set of historical circumstances that validate those themes, using the facts of history to explain Antonio's antipathy toward Shylock and make credible the cruelty of a legal system that would permit a creditor to take a pound of flesh.

46 *A Natural Perspective: The Development of Shakespearean Comedy and Romance* (San Diego: Harcourt, Brace, Jovanovich, n.d.), p. 41.

47 Bloom, *The Anxiety of Influence*, p. 94.

48 Bloom, *The Anxiety of Influence*, p. 94.

49 Frye, p. 51.

50 Frye, pp. 51-52.

51 Frye, p. 72.

52 Rowse, p. 37.

53 Donald R. Dudley, "Introduction," in *Roman Drama*, ed. T.A. Dorey and Donald R. Dudley (New York: Basic Books, 1965), p. vii. Also, Chute, p. 17: "Apart from learning to read Latin and write Latin, an English schoolboy was also expected to recite Latin, and here again was an aspect of the curriculum that might conceivably be of some use to a future actor. There was considerable emphasis on good public speaking and a controlled, intelligent use of the voice, and many schoolmasters let their boys act out Latin plays by Plautus and

Terence to give them experience in handling the spoken word."

54 *What Shakespeare Read and Thought*, p. 11.

55 William Allan Neilson and Ashley Horace Thorndike, *The Facts About Shakespeare* (New York: Macmillan & Co., 1961), p. 95.

56 Erich Segal, *Roman Laughter: The Comedy of Plautus*, Harvard Studies in Comparative Literature, 29 (Cambridge: Harvard University Press, 1968), p. 13. Also see pp. 7-14.

57 Segal quotes Sir James Frazer, p. 8.

58 Segal, pp. 13-14.

59 In *Masters of Ancient Comedy*, ed. and trans. by Lionel Casson (New York: Minerva Press, 1967), pp. 186-87 (I.20-33).

60 Segal, pp. 8-9. Segal notes, p. 177, that "there was never any drama associated with the Saturnalia in classical times... although it was the occasion for the revival of Roman comedies during the Renaissance."

61 Segal, p. 29.

62 Segal, p. 29.

63 Segal, p. 31.

64 Sylvan Barnet, in "Editor's introduction," in *Twentieth Century Interpretations of* The Merchant of Venice: *A Collections of Critical Essays*, p. 8.

65 *The Meaning of Shakespeare* (Chicago: University of Chicago Press, 1951), p. 112.

66 Goddard, p. 110. This passage is included in *William Shakespeare's* The Merchant of Venice, ed. Harold Bloom, pp. 34-35.

67 A comic reversal of fortune similar to Antonio's—a severe threat of death, suddenly turned into an opportunity for revenge against the enemy—is also found in the Bible's Book of Esther, which is recited in its entirety on the Jewish holiday of Purim, a holiday of masquerades, drinking and other festive excess, celebrated on a winter full-moon night. Those who argue that Portia should grant Shylock mercy, as she had asked him to do, should remember that comedy punishes the villains because comic literature obeys the laws of genre, not morality—a point that is as true for comic literature in the Bible as it is for Shakespearean comedy. As the Book of Esther states, "in the day that the enemies of the Jews hoped to have power over them; (though it was turned to the contrary, that the Jews had rule over them that hated them,) the Jews gathered themselves together in their cities... to lay hand on such as sought their hurt....Thus the Jews smote all their enemies with the stroke of the sword, and slaughter, and destruction, and did what they would unto those that hated them. And in Shushan the palace the Jews slew and destroyed five hundred men .... and the ten sons of Haman,...the enemy of the Jews, slew they" (9:1-10). Comic wish fulfillment quite obviously can be cruel to the oppressors—a festive inversion to the cruelty that the oppressors enforced in reality.

68 In contrast, in *Julius Caesar* Portia's confession of personal weakness

is a commitment to honor, rather than a concession to impulse: "O constancy, be strong upon my side;/ Set a huge mountain 'tween my heart and tongue!/ I have a man's mind, but a woman's might" (*JC*, II.iv.6-9).

69 Goddard, p. 112

70 Goddard, p. 112.

71 Goddard, p. 106.

72 Segal, pp. 53-54.

73 Segal, p. 15.

74 Among those who have made this point are Heine, pp. 673-74; and Girard, p. 91.

75 See the editor's introduction, p. lv, in the Arden edition of *The Merchant of Venice.*

76 Philip Edwards, *Shakespeare: A Writer's Progress* (Oxford: Oxford University Press, 1987), p. 100

77 In *Romeo and Juliet*, Romeo offers to swear upon the moon as a vow of fidelity to Juliet: "Lady, by yonder blessed moon I vow/ That tips with silver all these fruit-tree tops—." However, Juliet rejects this vow: "O, swear not by the moon, the inconstant moon,/ That monthly changes in her circled orb,/ Lest that thy love prove likewise variable" (II.ii.107-111).

78 Geary, p. 66.

79 Lyon, pp. 117-118.

80 Murray J. Levith, *Shakespeare's Italian Settings and Plays* (New York: St. Martin's Press, 1989), p. 17: "The ring Shylock had from his wife Leah smacks of the same magical foreigner stuff that Othello's handkerchief does."

81 Walter Kaufmann identifies this passage in Aristotle with Shakespeare's *Coriolanus* in *From Shakespeare to Existentialism* (Garden City, N.Y.: Doubleday & Co., Inc., 1960), p. 10. Also see *Ethica Nicomachea, The Works of Aristotle Translated into English*, 9 (London: Oxford Univ. Press, 1954), IV:3.

82 Charney, pp. 48-59, summarizes Shakespeare's use of the "imagery of blood" in *Julius Caesar.* "The central issue about the meaning of *Julius Caesar*," Charney writes, "is raised most forcefully and vividly by the imagery of blood," p. 48. For a contemporary, gender-sensitive interpretation of the "blood" and "bleeding" passages from *Julius Caesar*, see Gail Kern Paster, "'In the spirit of men there is no blood': Blood as Trope of Gender in *Julius Caesar*," in *Shakespeare's Early Tragedies: A Collection of Critical Essays*, ed. Mark Rose (Englewood Cliffs, N.J.: Prentice Hall, 1995), pp. 241-256.

83 Here is Plutarch's version of this story, as told in "The Life of Brutus," pp. 169-170: "This young lady being excellently well seen in philosophy, loving her husband well, and being of a noble courage, as she was also wise: because she would not ask her husband what he ailed before she had made some proof by herself, she took a little razor

such as barbers occupy to pare men's nails, and causing her maids and women to go out of her chamber, gave her self a great gash withal in her thigh, that she was straight all of a gore-blood, and incontinently after, a vehement fever took her, by reason of the pain of her wound.... she spoke in this sort to unto him: .... 'How may I show my duty towards thee, and how much I would do for thy sake, if I cannot constantly bear a secret mischance or grief with thee, which requireth secrecy and fidelity? I confess, that a woman's wit commonly is too weak to keep a secret safely: but yet, Brutus, good education and the company of virtuous men, have some power to reform the defect of nature. And for myself, I have this benefit moreover: that I am the daughter of Cato, and wife of Brutus. This notwithstanding, I did not trust to any of these things before: until that now I have found by experience, that no pain or grief whatsoever can overcome me.' With those words she showed him her wound on her thigh, and told him what she had done to prove her self. Brutus was amazed to hear what she said unto him, and lifting up his hands to heaven, he besought the gods to give him the grace he might bring his enterprise to so good pass, that he might be found a husband, worthy of so noble a wife as Porcia: so he then did comfort her the best he could."

84 Portia in *The Merchant of Venice* uses the word "blood" as a metaphor for passion—strong emotion that diverts her from sober commitments. She says: "the brain may devise laws for the blood, but a hot temper leaps o'er a cold decree" (1.2.17-19). In effect, she confesses that her hot blood usually overpowers cold rationality, which is exactly antithetical to the ethos of ancient Roman honor exemplified by Brutus and Portia in *Julius Caesar*. Bassanio also uses "blood" to mean emotion. When he is overwhelmed by the excitement of winning Portia's hand, he says: "Only my blood speaks to you in my veins,/ And there is such confusion in my powers" (3.2.176-177). For Brutus, integrity is backed by both flesh and blood; but Bassanio is governed by blood alone ("*only* my blood speaks to you," he says to Portia). His phrase "only my blood" is a mirror image opposite to Portia's stipulation that Shylock, who is devoid of all romantic passion, would be permitted to take a pound of flesh only, without the blood.

85 Lawrence Danson, in *The Harmonies of* The Merchant of Venice (New Haven: Yale University Press, 1978), p. 20n, quotes E.A.M. Colman, *The Dramatic Use of Bawdy in Shakespeare* (London, 1974), p. 77. Danson says the ring is "the visible sign of a sacramental union," as well as a word that can be used as a "bawdy pun—the bawdy significations of which are necessary to the fulfillment of the word's primary sacramental sense." Eric Partridge also identifies a ring with a bawdy pun on female genitals in *Shakespeare's Bawdy* (New York: E.P. Dutton & Co., Inc., 1960), p. 25 and p. 179. Geary. p. 67, also notes: "The ring in *The Merchant of Venice*—as well as being the symbol of the marriage contract—is similarly a comic sexual symbol."

86 Barber, p. 165. Also quoted in Bloom, p. 39.

87 Girard, p. 92.

88 Frye, p. 97, identifies Shylock as the idiotes character, like Malvolio, who is "misanthropic and opposed to festivity on principle." He defines this term, p. 93: "The idiotes is usually isolated from the action by being the focus of the anticomic mood, and so may be the technical villain, like Don John, or the butt, like Malvolio and Falstaff, or simply opposed by temperament to festivity, like Jaques. Although the villainous, the ridiculous, and the misanthropic are closely associated in comedy, there is enough variety of motivation here to indicate that the idiotes is not a character type, like the clown, through typical features recur, but a structural device that may use a variety of characters."

89 Frye, p. 72. Also see "The Triumph of Time," chapter III in *A Natural Perspective*, pp. 72-117.

90 Frye, p. 73.

91 Frye, pp. 74-75.

92 Frye, p. 76.

93 Frye, p. 76.

94 Frye, p. 78.

95 Frye, p. 79.

96 *The Merchant of Venice* directly precedes *As You Like It* in the First Folio edition of Shakespeare's work. Although it cannot be proven, it is possible that the two plays were placed next to each other in the Folio (by the First Folio editors, Shakespeare friends and colleagues John Heminge and Henry Condell) because it was understood that the two plays were closely related in some way, either chronologically or thematically.

97 See Gross, pp. 309-11, 329-30.

98 Segal, pp. 25-27.

99 Segal, p. 29.

100 In *Othello*, the manipulative Iago takes for granted the assumption that deception and marital infidelity are typical of Venice's moral environment: "I know our country disposition well;/ In Venice they do let Heaven see the pranks/ They dare not show their husbands. Their best conscience/ Is not to leave 't undone, but to keep 't unknown (*Oth.*, III.iii.201-204).

101 Geary, pp. 61-62, notes that *The Merchant of Venice* is unique in that "in no other Shakespearian comedy do the chief lovers meet for the first time so late in the play. This reflects the play's stress on the initial situation of the lovers: Portia bound by her father's will, and Bassanio in debt and virtually penniless. Bassanio's money troubles—a problem he shares with Jessica and Lorenzo—set him apart from the other romantic heroes of the comedies. Orsino, Benedick, Berowne, and the others never have to worry about finding money as Bassanio does.... But Bassanio, unable to manage his financial affairs efficiently, needs money, and the easiest and quickest way to get it is by finding himself a rich wife. The opening scene of the play establishes him as a fortune hunter."

102 Geary, p. 64.

103 Shakespeare uses the word "napkin" for Othello's handkerchief (*Oth.*, III.iii.287, 290, 321), which—like Orlando's bloody bandage—is also used as a symbolic measure of loyalty between a man and a woman. "Napkin" is used *in As You Like It*, (IV.iii.94, 155).

104 Goddard, p. 82.

105 Ironically, it is Desdemona's extreme fidelity to a vow—her rigid commitment to keep a promise "to the last article" (*Oth.*, III.iii.22)— that fuels Othello's suspicions that she has been unfaithful to him with Cassio. Desdemona persists in lobbying Othello on behalf of Cassio, not because she is in love with Cassio but because she is true—to the point of death, she says—to her concept of honor. She had said to Cassio: "Assure thee,/ If I do vow a friendship, I'll perform it to the last article. My lord shall never rest;/ I'll watch him tame, and talk him out of patience;/ His bed shall seem a school, his board a shrift;/ I'll intermingle everything he does/ With Cassio's suit. Therefore be merry, Cassio;/ For thy solicitor shall rather die/ Than give thy cause away" (*Oth.*, III.iii.20-28).

106 See the editor's notes in William Shakespeare, *The Merchant of Venice*, ed. John F. Andrews (London: J.M. Dent, 1991).

107 Iago, in *Othello*, also believes this proposition, which he utilizes in his campaign to destroy Othello: "When devils will the blackest sins put on,/ They do suggest at first with heavenly shows,/ As I do now" (*Oth.*, II.iii.357-359). Iago brings down Othello because he is able to manipulate Othello's tendency to mistake superficial appearance for the truth. "Men should be what they seem;/ Or those that be not, would they might seem none!," he says to Othello, who replies: "Certain, men should be what they seem" (*Oth.*, III.iii.127-128).

108 See Halio's introduction to The Oxford Shakespeare edition of *The Merchant of Venice*, p. 27.

109 Fiedler, pp. 87-88.

110 This ambiguous/complementary relationship between Shylock and Antonio is reflected in Professor Charlton's assertion that the epithet "fawning publican" should have been said by Antonio about Shylock, rather than by Shylock about Antonio, as it is in the play. Charlton, p. 139, says: "A generation ago, Moulton saw that 'fawning publican' would in every way be a proper description for Antonio to apply to Shylock."

111 Edwards, p. 101.

112 Girard, p. 93.

113 In a similar way, Iago is able to make himself appear honorable by speaking honestly of his own evil nature, telling Othello that "it is my nature's plague/ To spy into abuses, and oft my jealousy/ Shapes faults that are not" (*Oth.*, III.iii.146-148). But Othello interprets Iago's self-confessed character flaw as its opposite: as proof of Iago's sincerity, honesty and virtue. Iago therefore hides his evil nature by being open about it.

114 Nuttall, p. 282.

115 Nuttall, p. 282.

116 Bernard Grebanier notes the relation between Portia's use of the word "rack" and Bassanio's financial stake in her affection. When Bassanio tells Antonio of his need for money, Antonio says to him: "Try what my credit can in Venice do:/ That shall be rack'd even to the uttermost" (I.i.180-181). See Bernard Grebanier, *The Truth About Shylock* (New York: Random House, 1962), p. 9.

117 Like Bassanio, Othello, the Moor of Venice, also integrates the language of love and money. "Come, my dear love," Othello says to Desdemona. "The purchase made, the fruits are to ensue;/ The profit's yet to come 'tween me and you" (*Oth.*, II.iii.8-10).

118 Nuttall, p. 280.

119 Coriolanus' reference to "outward shows" implies that the phrase is synonymous with saying that appearance is false: "If these shows be not outward, which of you/ But is four Volsces?" (*Cor.*, I.vi.77).

120 Line 75 retains the punctuation of Folio and Quarto editions, as well as that of *The New Variorum Edition of Shakespeare*. More recent editions, including the Oxford Shakespeare, Arden and the Folger Library editions, substitute a comma for the colon in the middle of this line, eliminating a full stop in the middle of a long sentence.

121 See *The New Variorum Edition of Shakespeare*, ed. Horace Howard Furness (Philadelphia: Lippincott Co., 1892).

122 Danson, p. 184.

123 Danson, p. 185.

124 One exception is John F. Andrews in his editor's notes on this passage in *The Merchant of Venice* (London: J.M. Dent, 1991).

125 *The Dramatic Use of Bawdy in Shakespeare* (London: Longman, 1974).

126 Danson, p. 185.

127 In addition to the Oxford Shakespeare, other modern editions with this word change are: the Arden edition edited by John Russell Brown, the Riverside edition of Shakespeare edited by G. Blakemore Evans; The Complete Oxford Shakespeare with *The Merchant* edited by William Montgomery, general editors Stanley Wells and Gary Taylor (Oxford: Clarendon Press, 1988); the New Cambridge edition edited by William Allan Neilson and Charles Jarvis Hill (Boston: Houghton Mifflin Co., 1970); the New Folger Library edition, edited by Barbara Mowat and Paul Werstine (New York: Washington Square Press, 1992); the Pelican Shakespeare, edited by Brents Stirling (New York: Penguin, 1987); the Bantam paperback edition edited by Donald Bevington (New York: Bantam, 1980); and the Signet paperback edition edited by Kenneth Myrick (New York: Signet (Penguin), 1965). Two exceptions are the versions edited respectively by John F. Andrews (London: J.M. Dent & Co., 1991) and A.L. Rowse (New York: Clarkson N. Potter, 1978).

128 *The Merchant of Venice*, eds. Louis B. Wright and Virginia LaMar,

(New York: Washington Square Press, 1968).

129 M.M. Mahood, ed. *The Merchant of Venice* (Cambridge: Cambridge Univ. Press, 1987).

130 Danson, p. 138,

131 Sigurd Burckhardt, "*The Merchant of Venice*: The Gentle Bond," *ELH*, 29, No. 3 (September, 1962), p. 255.

132 R. Chris Hassell, Jr., "Antonio and the Ironic Festivity of *The Merchant of Venice*," *Shakespeare Studies*, 6 (1972), p. 69.

133 A.D. Nuttall, "The Merchant of Venice," in *William Shakespeare: Comedies & Romances,* ed. Harold Bloom (New York: Chelsea House Publishers, 1986), p. 282: Nuttall defines "kidding on the level" as a: "conversational practice known in the slang of forty years ago ... the speaker makes a remark which sounds ironic but the real joke lies in the fact that every word is literally intended: 'Hello darling, you know I hate your guts.'"

134 Lyon, pp. 121-122.

135 Robert Ornstein, *Shakespeare's Comedies: From Roman Farce to Romantic Mystery* (Newark: University of Delaware Press, 1986), p. 90.

136 For a discussion of constancy as an attribute of noble Romans, see Geoffrey Miles, *Shakespeare and the Constant Romans* (Oxford: Clarendon Press, 1996). Miles discusses in depth North's Plutarch and *Julius Caesar, Coriolanus, and Antony and Cleopatra.* See especially pp. 110-122.

137 Plutarch, p. 169.

138 Miles devotes a chapter to *Julius Caesar*, pp. 123-148.

139 Plutarch, p. 117-118.

140 Kaufmann, in *From Shakespeare to Existentialism*, pp. 11-17, identifies antagonism between the great mass of people and the noble individual as an issue common to several Shakespeare plays, including *Julius Caesar, Coriolanus, Hamlet, Timon of Athens* and *Troilus and Cressida.*

141 Shylock fumes "My own flesh and blood to rebel!" (3.1.32) in reaction to his daughter's escape. Solanio's replies: "Rebels it at these years?" (III.i.32).

142 Plutarch, p. 130.

143 Levin, p. 190.

144 Segal, pp. 11-12.

145 Levin, p. 190, notes the contrast between Antony and Coriolanus: "Plutarch, the Greek moralist, saw Coriolanus as an outstanding example of the peculiarly Roman conception of virtue: .... Plutarch's contrasting parallel is the career of Alcibiades, whose ingratiating suppleness—like Antony's—throws the intransigent arrogance of Coriolanus into bold relief."

146 In this respect, *The Merchant of Venice* is similar to James Joyce's *Ulysses*: both Shylock and Bloom could be considered literary ex-

amples of metempsychosis—a classical hero reborn or transposed into mundane modernity. Both are an historical anachronism, representing ideals that in another context would be noble and lofty. But although Ulysses is a great hero in Homer, his legendary greatness is compromised by the pettiness of his environment when he finds himself in the persona of Leopold Bloom in 1904 June 16 Dublin; likewise, Hercules, the ancient hero to whom Portia compares Bassanio—and who was claimed as an ancestor by Antony, the literary forbear to Bassanio's noble kinsman, Antonio—would be out of place in the Jewish ghetto of Venice. Consequently, both Shylock and Bloom could be considered a comic inverse of a classical ideal: both are ostensibly Jews (though with obscure issues of identity). Both suffer a violation of the family bond. And their dignity suffers in the comic context defined for them in *The Merchant of Venice* and *Ulysses* respectively.

In *Ulysses*, the character Martin Cunningham has a "resemblance to Shakespeare," according to Hugh Kenner in *Ulysses* (Baltimore: The Johns Hopkins Univ. Press, 1987), p. 103. "And he [Cunningham] has devised for Bloom a role modelled on Shylock's." In the context of an interpretation of *The Merchant of Venice* based on the honor/irony paradigm, Bloom becomes an historical anachronism several times over: first, as a displaced Ulysses; and second, as a displaced Shylock, who—in turn—may have been a displaced Roman noble. I don't wish to imply that Joyce in any way validates my interpretation of *The Merchant of Venice*. My point is merely that Shakespeare is just as capable as Joyce of playing games with canonical literature, thereby adding an additional level to Joyce's irony when Shakespeare becomes Joyce's subject matter.

147 David C. McPherson, *Shakespeare, Jonson, and the Myth of Venice* (Cranbury, N.J.: Associated University Presses, 1990), p. 94.

148 McPherson, p. 94.

149 Quoted by McPherson, p. 94. The bracketed material inserted within this quotation is McPherson's.

150 McPherson, p. 94.

151 McPherson, p. 95.

152 McPherson, p. 94.

153 Niccolo Machiavelli, *Discourses on the First Ten Books of Titus Livius*, translated by Christian E. Detmold (New York: The Modern Library, 1950), p. 106.

154 McPherson, p. 136.

155 McPherson, p. 36. Also see Vaughan, pp. 15-16.

156 McPherson, p. 37.

157 McPherson, p. 40.

158 Levith, pp. 12-15. Also see Virginia Mason Vaughan, *Othello: A Contextual History* (Cambridge: Cambridge Univ. Press, 1994), pp. 16-17.

159 Levith, p. 18.

160 William Thomas, as quoted in Levith, p. 12.

161 Levith, pp. 12-13.

162 See chapter the previous chapter "Debt and Desire."

163 Plutarch, p. 127.

164 Plutarch, p. 106.

165 Plutarch, pp. 109-110.

166 Plutarch, pp. 116-117.

167 Plutarch, pp. 104-105.

168 In stating that a poem should only be reduced to another poem because "the meaning of a poem can only be another poem," Professor Bloom contends that "this is not a tautology, not even a deep tautology, since the two poems are not the same poem, any more than two lives can be the same life" (*The Anatomy of Influence*, p. 94.) However, to extend Bloom's logic, it may indeed be tautological to reduce a poem to itself (rather than to another poem). If (as Bloom says) it is not a tautology to reduce one poem to another poem because it is impossible for two poems to be the same poem, then conversely, a single poem reduced to itself could be twofold and therefore tautological.

169 As recapitulated by Gary Taylor, in *Reinventing Shakespeare: A Cultural History from the Restoration to the Present* (New York: Weidenfeld & Nicolson, 1989), p. 329. Taylor cites an unpublished paper delivered at the Twenty-second International Shakespeare Conference on August 21, 1986 by Booth, a professor at the University of California at Berkeley.

170 As quoted by Taylor, p. 329.

171 Taylor quotes Booth, pp. 329-330.

172 As quoted by Taylor, p. 329.

173 Elton, p. 17.

174 Elton, pp. 17-18.

175 Elton, p. 27.

176 Elton, p. 24.

177 Elton, p. 27.

178 Elton, p. 17.

179 Elton, p. 32.

180 Elton, p. 32.

181 Kermode, p. 225.

182 Kermode, p. 224.

183 *The Western Canon*, pp. 8-9.

184 Levin, p. 54.

185 J. Middleton Murry, "Shakespeare's Method: *The Merchant of Venice*," in *Shakespeare: The Comedies; A Collection of Critical Essays*, p. 39.

186 Middleton Murry, p. 39.

187 Middleton Murry, p. 44

188 Goddard, pp. viii-ix.

189 Charlton, pp. 127-135.

190 "Introduction," in *William Shakespeare: Comedies and Romances*, ed. Harold Bloom (New York: Chelsea House Publishers, 1986), p. 2.

191 See Danson, pp. 270-275.

192 Danson, pp. 270-271.

193 Danson, p. 351.

194 Coriolanus notes the tendency of extreme hate and extreme love to quickly invert their positions:

> O world, thy slippery turn! Friends now fast sworn,
> Whose double bosoms seem to wear one heart,
> Whose heart, whose bed, whose meal and exercise
> Are still together, who twin, as 'twere, in love
> Unseparable, shall within this hour,
> On a dissension of a doit, break out
> To bitterest enmity; so fellest foes
> Whose passions and whose plots have broke their sleep
> To take the one the other, by some chance,
> Some trick not worth an egg, shall grow dear friends
> And interjoin their issues.   (*Cor.*, IV.iv.12-22)

195 See René Girard, *Shakespeare: A Theater of Envy*, p. 19.

196 The terms "thesis," "antithesis" and synthesis are used here for illustrative purposes only, not in the exact manner defined by Fichte and Schelling. For more background on these terms, see Walter Kaufmann, *Hegel: A Reinterpretation* (Garden City, N.Y.: Doubleday, 1966), p. 154; also, see George Lichtheim, *Marxism: An Historical and Critical Study*, second revised edition (New York: Praeger Publishers, 1965), pp. 7-10.

197 Coolidge, p. 243. See above, chapter 1., "Cultural paradigms, critical premises."

198 A.L. Rowse, in his annotations to *The Merchant of Venice*, comments that "crisped snaky golden locks" is reminiscent of a fashion favored by Venetian courtesans, who were portrayed by the Venetian painters with crimped gold hair. See *The Annotated Shakespeare, Vol. I, The Comedies*, ed. A.L. Rowse (New York: Clarkson N. Potter, 1978), p. 309.

199 McPherson, p 46.

200 Colman, p. 222, cross-references *Much Ado About Nothing* (I.i.274), where Don Pedro says: "If Cupid had not spent all his quiver in Venice, thou wilt quake for this shortly."

201 McPherson, p. 43.

202 McPherson, p. 45.

203 McPherson, p. 46. Also, see Levith, pp. 13-14.

204 McPherson, p. 39.

About the Author

Robert Schneider has written thousands of published articles in a 20-year-career in journalism and corporate communications. He wrote by-lined articles and columns in his capacity as a news reporter, business writer and business editor; in his capacity as a public relations manager, he published numerous ghost-written pieces in the trade journals of various industries, including healthcare, education, state government and electronics. He has extensive experience as an executive speech writer, and has been the editor-in-chief and manager of marketing publications for several Fortune 100 corporations. Currently Mr. Schneider is the editor-in-chief of Compaq Computer's global intranet publication, *news.CPQ*.

He holds a B.A. degree from The Johns Hopkins University (1974), where he studied comparative literature and languages. His M.A. degree is from Columbia University (1975), where he studied the cultural history of modern Europe.